Praise for Jean Houston's *Mystical Dogs*

"If you have picked up this book, chances are that you already know the sweet and tender grace of the doggy-human bond. But do we take care of them, or are they the ardent tutors of our own emerging consciousness? Read and be delighted."

—Joan Borysenko, Ph.D., author of
Minding the Body, Mending the Mind

"Jean Houston's *Mystical Dogs* makes us realize how profoundly our beloved pets can keep us in touch with the oneness that is Nature and Divinity. All this and lots of chuckles."

—Marion Woodman, author of
Addiction to Perfection and *Coming Home to Myself*

"No one can take a simple story of a man saying good-bye to his beloved dog and turn it into a striking metaphor about personal and planetary transformation as seamlessly, insightfully and delightfully as Jean Houston. As is the case of every true genius, Houston sees all of life with the eyes of the soul. Gifts of gifts, she then translates for the rest of us in a way that expands our minds, touches our hearts, and allows our own souls to breathe again. Fresh air for the suffocating soul—that is what Jean Houston is. Savor her latest work, *Mystical Dogs*."

—Neale Donald Walsch, author of
Conversations with God

"A few years ago a shaman instructed me that the 4-legged ones were so concerned about us 2-leggeds that they were having conferences about how they might help us. *Mystical Dogs* speaks to that deep truth: We are not alone in the universe and other creatures and spirits assist us. If only we would listen, and listen as deeply as Jean Houston has in this book."

—Matthew Fox, author of
Original Blessing and *One River, Many Wells*

"This brave, generous, passionate book will confirm in their truth, those who love animals and know them to be wise and holy. And it will awaken all those who are not yet aware to the miraculous companionship nature has to offer all those willing to risk the adventure."

—Andrew Harvey, author of
The Direct Path and *The Return of the Mother*

"Jean Houston reminds us of the eternal wisdom, high play, heart companionship and simple joy of life in *Mystical Dogs.* From Rin Tin Tin to the Hounds of Heaven, we all need to be refreshed daily with the ever-constant love that barks, marks and shares the best of life with us. You'll remember the loving eyes of your own mystical companions as you read this charmed book."

—Don Campbell, author of
The Mozart Effect

"The unique and extraordinary role dogs (and cats) have played in human life has been the subject of much creative expression throughout the millennia. Jean Houston has discovered what other cultures have known about our spiritual friends. They are essentially *custos animi,* guardians of our souls. In this delightful, powerful, entertaining, but seriously illuminating book, she takes us beyond dogs as simply affectionate property of humans, to spiritual guides, being capable of genuine spiritual friendship with us, vehicles of divine guidance and selfless love, carriers of unitive experience and ecstatic joy. *Mystical Dogs* is a great gift for the spiritual life in our times, and an important teaching of the value of sentience beyond our often anthropocentric predicament."

—Wayne Teasdale, author of
The Mystic Heart and *A Monk in the World*

"Only as magnificent of a human potential teacher as Jean Houston could have the insight and humility to recognize the dogs in her life as high spiritual teachers. No reader will forget the Madonna Chickie, great and gentle Titan, and others up to the fine angel Luna, as Houston explains their teachings on all eight stages of the spiritual path. Reading this book gem, you will recognize your own canine companion (or other pet) as the true teacher in your own life or rush out to meet one anew."

—Elisabet Sahtouris, evolution biologist, futurist,
author of *Earthdance*

"Jean Houston has done it again! After her ground-breaking research into states of consciousness with her husband, Robert Masters, she now explores a new area, one that pet lovers have glimpsed and indigenous peoples have known for millennia, where animals serve as companions and guides for humans on their own spiritual journey into the higher realms of consciousness."

—Ewert Cousins, general editor of
World Spirituality: An Encyclopedic History of the Religious Quest

"*Mystical Dogs* will change forever your view of dogs, and guide you with clarity and grace through the stages of your spiritual journey. Using her love affair with these exceptional animals as her spiritual mentors, and drawing on her vast knowledge of human consciousness, Jean Houston has written a warm, wonderful, clear and readable book on the potential of us all to evolve systematically to ever-higher levels of consciousness and union with the Divine. I recommend it to everyone with a spiritual yearning."

—Harville Hendrix, Ph.D., author of
Getting the Love You Want
and Helen Hunt, coauthor of
Giving the Love that Heals

Books by Jean Houston

Jump Time:
Shaping Your Future in a World of Radical Change

A Passion for the Possible:
A Guide to Realizing Your True Potential

A Mythic Life:
Learning to Live Our Greater Story

Manual for the Peacemaker:
An Iroquois Legend to Heal Self & Society

Public Like a Frog:
Entering the Lives of Three Great Americans

The Hero and the Goddess

Life Force:
The Psycho-Historical Recovery of the Self

Godseed:
The Journey of Christ

The Search for the Beloved:
Journeys in Sacred Psychology

The Possible Human

Mind Games:
The Guide to Inner Space

The Passion of Isis and Osiris

Mystical
Dogs

"Come in! Come in!" cried the gatekeeper.
"You have been faithful to the end and so has your dog.
Your dog is a living example of the dharma, the way of truth.
He has been with you always. Come in. Come."
And the great king and his dog entered Paradise.

Mystical Dogs

ANIMALS AS GUIDES TO OUR INNER LIFE

Jean Houston

INNER
OCEAN

Inner Ocean Publishing, Inc.
P.O. Box 1239
Makawao, Maui, HI 96768-1239

Cover design: Bill Greaves
Cover photo: Stone
Interior page design: Bill Greaves
Interior page typography: Madonna Gauding
Editing: Barbara Doern Drew

Publisher Cataloging-in-Publication Data

Houston, Jean.
       Mystical dogs : animals as guides to our
    inner life / Jean Houston. - -Makawao, HI :
    Inner Ocean, 2002.

          p. ; cm.
    ISBN 1-930722-13-3
          1. Dogs. 2. Dogs - -Religious aspects. 3.
    Dogs - -Mythology. 4. Dogs - -Folklore. I.
    Title.

SF426 .H68 2002
636.7002 - -dc21   CIP

Printed in Canada by Friesens

9 8 7 6 5 4 3 2 1

CONTENTS

To all my dogs:
Chickie, Champ, Oliver, Titan, Moondog,
Zingua, Barnaby, Saji, Burton, Luna, and Zeus.

ACKNOWLEDGMENTS

First and foremost, thanks go to the dogs, all those glorious canine friends who have allowed me to share their lives—Chickie, Champ, Titan, Oliver, Moondog, Zingua, Barnaby, Burton, Luna, Zeus, and Dr. Joy's Nova. Without the years spent with them, life would have been much less than it has been and this book would not be at all.

I am grateful to John Nelson, editorial director of Inner Ocean Publishing, for his fine sense of how this book should unfold. He offered wise and salient advice in the midst of his prodigious activities in helping to create a new company. I want to especially thank him for putting me in the hands of an extraordinary editor, Barbara Doern Drew. She not only shares a soul connection to dogs, but is spiritually wise and adept in her understanding of the stages of the mystic path. I also want to thank her children and husband for allowing me to take up so much of her time. Mom's back, folks, and dog lovers everywhere are beholden to you.

My good friend and associate Peggy Rubin offered many hours of practical help in the writing of the final chapters. A special blessing is that Peggy also knew more than half of the dogs in this book, and her memories of each of them added much to the stories here. Additionally, as coteacher in our seminars on spiritual development, she brings her remarkable scholarship to bear on the spiritual pathways explored here.

I want to thank my brother, Robert Houston, for his sharing of memories and photos of the dogs who graced our early years. Fonda Joyce offered juicy recollections as well. Thanks go to Lucienne Estes and to her tiny but powerful Yorkshire terrier, Bridget, who came to work with her mistress each day and stood her own as part of the unlikely pack with Luna and Zeus, each of whom outweighs her by more than twenty times. Another Bridget,

Bridget Reynolds, our general manager, plays Hera to our Zeus and keeps our Olympian household in order. Much ongoing gratitude to her.

Again, as with my other books, Elisabeth Zinck Rothenberger has transcribed the original presentation of this material as it was given in my mystery school sessions.

My husband, Robert Masters, has enriched this book with his special understanding and shared memories of the dogs who have graced our life together.

And gratitude goes to the many friends who have shared the stories of the remarkable dogs in their lives. I've found that if you start telling dog stories, it opens up an unquenchable river of memories, mad and merry tales, and, above all, remembrances so poignant as to draw tears as well as laughter.

INTRODUCTION

The Mystery of Mystical Dogs

Like many of you, I love animals, dogs especially. For much of my life, whenever I am home, I am rarely more than three feet away from fur. Dogs are the friends of my soul; I fall into their eyes and know utter contentment. I have found that a great many of my ideas and knowings have been accompanied by the presence and, often, the inspiration of dogs. Dogs have given me steady emotional support and frequently in circumstances that my fellow humans have regarded as fraught with ambiguity. When I have taken an action that no one has understood, and relatives and friends have thought I was crazy or just way off track, a dog has barked encouragement or shown with a paw to my hand that I was sufficient just for my being there. Whether I've been down in the dumps or ecstatic with joy, dogs have matched my mood with sympathy and celebration. But then, too, in the very ordinary parts of my life, dogs are ever near, head on knee, lying on foot, offering an ordinary, extraordinary grace. Look in their eyes and you find beatitude; listen to the thumping of their tail when you come through the door and you know that you are well met in this curious universe of ours.

Dogs are the great companions of our lives. They teach us, love us, care for us even when we are uncaring, feed our souls, and always, always give us the benefit of the doubt. With natural grace, they give us insight into the nature of the good and often provide us with a mirror of our better nature, as well as a remembrance of once and future possibilities. Foolishly we too often regard them as an inferior species—our poor, if much loved, relation. And in that we are wrong.

A man wise in the ways of animals, nature writer Henry Beston, once wrote:

We need another and a wiser and perhaps a more mythical con-
cept of animals. . . . We patronize them for their incompleteness,
for their tragic fate of having taken form so far below ourselves.
And therein we err, and greatly err. For the animal shall not be
measured by man. In a world older and more complete than ours
they moved finished and complete, gifted with extensions of the
senses we have lost or never attained, living by voices we shall
never hear. They are not brethren, they are not underlings; they
are other nations, caught with ourselves in the net of life and
time, fellow prisoners of the splendor and travail of the earth.[1]

I think of the most ancient of peoples crawling through the
chilling darkness and fearful turnings of deep, deep caves there in
northern Spain and southern France, pulling themselves up on a
shelf of rock, there to mix their blood with ground stone pigments
and the fat of a kill, there to paint by the light of a torch the wonder of animals seen and remembered.

How perfect are these renditions in Altamira, in Lascaux, in
the cave known as the "Trois Frères"—how powerful in beauty and
form and sheer such-ness of being. I was fortunate to be one of the
last people to see the actual Lascaux cave before it was closed to the
public. Captured there on the rock are forms in flight—mammoth
and bison, antelope and dog—in full magnificence and the mystery of their power. Juxtaposed with these, in the corner is a little
stick figure of a human, bereft of magic—a poor relation, unhoofed,
untoothed, untailed, disenchanted, lost. But able, nevertheless, to
descend into sacred darkness and there in this underworld temple
of rock to remember and recapture.

To recapture what? Experts tell us that they were trying to
paint as perfect a portrait of these much admired beasts as possible

as an act of sympathetic magic that would help them in the hunt. Perhaps, in part, but probably not entirely. For what was the overriding emotion that stirred such efforts, such artistic genius? It was awe—awe before the presence of those who were still part of the sacred flow of nature. To me, those early pictures show the desperation of those who were forgetting their connection. As we raised our snouts from off the ground and searched the sky, we in some sense lost our bearings. And there were no skyhooks to hang on to. Our frontal lobes multiplied and burgeoned connections leading to constructions—law, art, religion, justice, hierarchy, abstractions from the ground of being—and we looked again at animals to remember what we had lost.

Down the millennia we turned them into gods, hoping to capture their fierce presence in our now once-removed spirituality. The Egyptians promoted this ambiguity by giving them animal heads on human bodies: cow-headed Hathor, goddess of love; jackal-headed Anubis, god of transformations and mysteries; ibis-headed Thoth, god of wisdom and magic; lionness-headed Sekhmet, goddess of healing, of magic, of justified rage, and of the unspoken mysteries. Throughout the world, animals have inspired and have been the focus of our spiritual yearnings: among the Maya, the jaguar; among the Celts, the bull; among the Minoans, the snake. Archaic peoples observed the ways in which animals surpassed human capacities and powers and made of them animal totems, tribal symbols, and even gods. Many peoples the world over have as essential parts of their creation myths the story of the birth of humanity from an animal or creature—a snake, a turtle, a raven— knowing in some primal way that we are descended of them and that is why perhaps they became our first gods.

I have been in Australia and observed as an Aboriginal woman of the emu totem entered into the body, mind, and spirit of the great bird so totally that for an instant her human form disappeared into the bird form. There was no emu present for her to imitate, but she had so closely identified with her totem that every movement and gesture had become emu and nothing but emu. And whereas, previously, this woman had been silent and withdrawn, for a time afterward she became vocal and expressive and taught us much. When I asked her how this had happened, she told me, "I caught my Dreaming—I was my ancestor." She had become her totem and through it had dropped the demeaning projections placed upon an urban-ghetto Aborigine. So many of the indigenous societies I have visited and worked with have kept up or, in many cases, recovered their animal, totemic life. By ritually enacting and identifying with their clan totem, they regain courage and strength and even wisdom lost in their human experience.

Plato wrote of how things are both here and there: here in this concrete world of space and time, and there in the world of essence, the archetypal realm, where the great patterns for all things are held. In the archetypal world these concrete realities bear their ideal form, and it is that form that gives things their continuity, their assurance of being, their wholeness and holiness. All animals have an archetypal form; thus, all animals have their wholeness. We humans seem to be the only ones without a clear guiding archetype. Ours are blended, confused, partaking of different eras and the accretions acquired by way of our various diaspora. This is why in many indigenous societies people take the animal as their heavenly double.

What is one of the most successful enterprises in the world today? By any economic or populist standard it is the various Disney worlds where archetypal animals—Mickey the Mouse, Donald the

Duck, Goofy the Dog—are there to greet us and bring us home again to a land of wonder and enchantment. The creators of Disneyland and Disney World may not know it, but they have presented us with modern Platonic forms, and in their presence we feel safe and ready for adventure.

I once had a conversation at Disneyland in California with a man who every day and for some time had worn the Mickey Mouse costume. He had divested himself of costume and mask, and now was permitted to talk. I asked him what it was like being Mickey Mouse month after month, and he told me something very strange. He said that sometimes when he looked into the eyes of wonder of some little child, he felt that he was the great Mouse and that he also was the essence of the heart and spirit and knowledge of all animals. Then the parent of the child would tell him to pose for the camera and it would be gone. But for a moment, he had known the magic and the mystery that indigenous people know when playing in their totemic incarnation.

Animals seem to live in another domain of time and space, one that transcends our clocks and mappings. Maybe because they do not read the maps they can find us across thousands of miles and in spite of impossible odds. They seem to be able to pick up on the broadcast beam of their beloved humans. There is the well-known story of Bobbie, a collie who had somehow been abandoned in Indiana but found his way back to Oregon and his home, a distance of some 3000 miles. A reporter who traced his route found plenty of people who had helped him and discovered as well that he had taken the shortest and most direct route. And there is Sugar, a Persian cat with a distinctive hip deformity, who traveled 1400 miles from Anderson, California, to his owners' home in Gage, Oklahoma.

One of my dogs was once picked up by strangers on a road she was traveling. She either escaped their car or was dropped off about a hundred miles from home. We knew it was that far because a teenager involved in the "pickup" had had a guilty conscience, had read the phone number on our pet's collar, and had called us with the news. Somehow our dog managed to find her way back days later, weary and filled with burrs and leaves sticking to her fur. She collapsed gratefully at our feet and did not rise again for twelve hours except to lap up several bowls of water that we placed under her willing jaws.

Some of our reverence before animals is that they seem to belong to some eternal time beyond time. They are both punctual, meaning living here and now, and durative, that is, having an eternal life. Each animal that we have known is, in some way, not dead, even though we may have attended their dying. Perhaps this is so because of their symbolic powers in our lives, their ability to relate us again and again or, if you will, bridge us again and again to the great space/time universal realm in which our local space and time are nested, or are but tributaries.

The anthropologist Claude Levy Strauss once said that among certain indigenous people the totem animal is regarded in awe not only because it is good to eat, but because it is "good to think" and to hold in the imagination. Animals give us much of our imaginal life; they inhabit our imaginations. How often do you dream of animals, have visionary experiences that involve animals, follow pathways into inner space guided by animals? Animals stretch our boundaries, prompt us to ask great questions again of ourselves and of existence. And, ultimately, they restore us to the fold of life. As German poet Rainer Maria Rilke observed in the first elegy of his poetic masterpiece, *Duino Elegies*, "We are not at home in this interpretative world" (translation mine).[2] Animals, by contrast, require no priest, no interpreter, to put them back in touch with their power, their freedom, their strength, fleetness, beauty, endurance, and capacities.

It is thus because they possess their power that we can invest them with the concentrated intensity of the symbol. Since time out of mind, we two-leggeds have performed symbolic ceremonies in order to regain our continuity with nature, masking ourselves as animals, enacting their postures, imitating their movements. Symbols and the rituals that contain them offer the possibility of aligning with nature's powers with consequences that can seem miraculous. I have been witness to the Navaho kachina ceremonies as they take on the headdress of the cloud-bearer who is to bring the rain. And even if the sky is blue and cloudless, you had better bring an umbrella! Likewise, to dance in the costume of the eagle is to engage the power of vision, the nobility of purpose. Thus the animal, in all times and places, has served as one who points the way to a higher way of being and restores us to partnership with nature.

As we have moved into cities, burdened ourselves with artifacts, extended our bodies and minds into machines, gotten our thrills from watching the screen and not having the experience, and thus become progressively isolated, alienated, and angsted, we have departed from the real knowledge of the world. As a result, animals have become ever more important as our guides and allies—the ones who bring us home to life.

There is a legend that is attached to the story of the expulsion of Adam and Eve in the Garden of Eden, which says that as they were leaving, certain animals, the dog and the cat in particular, decided to follow the human couple into their exile. They agreed to be partners to the exiles, both then and forever afterward, loving companions who would share our lives and serve as our teachers and beloveds.

It is thus with animals that we could forget the long night of exile and remember who we really were as earth-spawned "Godseeds." They are the ones who have the uncanny way of allowing us while in their presence to drop and discard the false layers of accumulated life and let our true minds and true hearts shine through. They have become our familiars, our "attendant spirits." They have become our confidantes and teachers because they remember the original instructions given them by an ancient universe. Storyteller Joseph Bruchac suggested in one of his sessions I once attended that animals are wiser than human beings because they do not forget how to behave. He said, "A bear never forgets it is a bear, yet human beings often forget what a human must do. Humans forget to take care of their families and forget to show respect to other things. They become confused because of material possessions and power."

Whenever I lose perspective—forget what is real and what is not—I look at the sleeping cat in the sun, who gives me the gentle reminder to slow down, relax, enjoy life. Whenever I stew about the world scene and the important place I occasionally delude myself into thinking I hold in it, I look into the eyes of Luna, my white German shepherd, who presents me with her paw to connect me back to what is really important: friendship, love, the greater life of which we are a part. No matter what we experience of all the profound and deep heartbreaks that may come our way, our pets, especially our dogs and cats, have a quality of steadiness that is always there for us and offer an invitation to life's fullness that may have been forgotten.

Then, too, animal spirits call us forth out of our old ways of being and into more abundant living—the celebration of what is. What is more, they give us keys to the greatest of human journeys: the path of awakening to the larger life. Is it any wonder, then, that the sense of the numinous shines from the figures of these animals in the old cave paintings, or that the great archetypal gods and goddesses of ancient times were often accompanied by a dog in their tasks of healing or leading the prepared initiate into higher realms of consciousness? The ancients knew what we are yet discovering: that dogs are holy guides to the unseen worlds.

Since early in my years on Earth, I have lived what can only be called a mythic life (the title, by the way, of my autobiography). I have worked in the field of exploring the nature of latent human capacities and of finding ways of applying these to education, human and social development, and spiritual life as well. As teacher, lecturer, and codirector of The Foundation for Mind Research, I have engaged in this work in more than a hundred countries. Giving seminars, teaching in my own "mystery school," and working in different cultures with international development agencies has given me the good fortune of learning from some of the most remarkable people of our time, many of whom are unknown and all of whom are a blessing to this planet.

But, looking closer to home, I have realized that some of my greatest teachings have come from my beloved canine companions. I wanted to offer a tribute to them, an acknowledgment of their role and significance relative to human development and in particular of their role in my life. I decided to try to find a form that would make these not just a collection of "sweet dog stories" but something of greater import for our human lives: their role as exemplars and guides to spiritual life, even to the stages of the mystical path.

To some, this equating of the mystical experiences and dogs may seem foolish, even sacrilegious. "*Mystical Dogs*??!" a friend of mine exclaimed in some heat when I told her the title of the book I was planning to write. "That's nonsense. How can you possibly put mysticism and dogs together? It's like putting rabbits and football in the same group, or elephants and space stations, or . . ."

She began to search for ever more impossible duos when I interrupted, "Have you ever had a dog?"

"No," she admitted. "My parents wouldn't let me. Once I brought home a puppy from a friend whose dog had fifteen babies, but they made me give him back. And then I grew up living in the city and all . . ."

"Geraldine! What do you think your life would have been like had you been allowed to keep that puppy?" I challenged. "Just do me a favor and imagine being seven or eight and having this dog for your companion."

Geraldine, who is noted for her imaginative gifts, thought for a moment and then said, "Well, I do have some idea, come to think of it. I used to visit an aunt and uncle on their farm. They had three kids and several dogs, and we'd go running together. But if I had had my own dog, well . . . I think I would have had entry into another world. I would have had a different kind of playmate, one with whom I wouldn't have had to be so careful about what I said or did. I would not have been so locked up in myself. I would have played with my dog in his world—learned to bark, rolled around in the grass with him, had secret places that only he and I would have known. I would have touched him a lot, and he would have brushed up on me, wanting to be patted or scratched.

"We would have had all kinds of adventures," she continued. "He would have taken me into dog world. We would have gone wild together. We would have run and run until we were exhausted and then lain panting in the sun, having experienced the elements. The power of our physical bodies would have felt so alive, so full of possibility, and yet one with everything. And then we'd have figured out some more games to play.

"As I'd follow my dog as he went snooping around, I would have been more alert to the sights and sounds around us," Geraldine visualized further. "I would have gotten something of dog mind and senses. And at night he would have curled up with me in bed and we would have awoken together, his cold nose poking at me to get up and have wonderful new adventures. I would have sneaked food to him from my plate, and we would have shared secrets and special games. If I was unhappy he'd have been there with me, trying to make it all right. We would have been great friends—best friends. And I would have known what it is to love totally and to be completely loved in turn."

What Geraldine was unwittingly describing were some of the stages of the classical spiritual journey, the road that mystics of all times and places have taken in their pursuit of the larger reality. We have been on journeys with dogs for thousands of years, as hunters, companions of the road, friends at the hearth. But if you look at the nature of this companionship, it goes far beyond the platitudes of a boy and his dog. It is a mystery that shakes paws with the infinite and guides us to the farther shore of our nature's highest promise.

For what is mysticism but the art of union with Reality, and a mystic, a person who aims at and believes in the attainment of such union. In its classical spiritual form it is a heroic journey, and valiant efforts are required to follow the path. Many of the spiritual teachers of the world have likened our lives to "a sleep and a forgetting." The mystic path, rather, is predicated on awakening, on going off robot and abandoning lackluster passivity to engage cocreation with vigor, attention, focus, and radiance, characteristics we might note we often find in our animal friends.

Thus the mystical experience is perhaps the greatest accelerator of evolutionary enhancement. Through it, we tap into wider physical, mental, and emotional systems, thereby gaining entrance into the next stage of our unfolding, both individually and collectively. Once the province of the few, the mystic path may now be the requirement of the many—a unique developmental path for self and world.

In a lifetime of studying the art and science of human development, I have found no more powerful, practical, and evolutionary practice than what is known as the mystic path. When I have studied or talked with seekers who have had this experience, they have told me of a joy that passes understanding, an immense surge of creativity, an instant uprush of kindness and tolerance that makes them impassioned champions for the betterment of all, bridge builders, magnets for solutions, peacemakers, pathfinders. Best of all, other people feel enriched and nourished around them. Everyone they touch becomes more because they themselves *are* more. Perhaps we have needed the changes and accelerations of our time to put the flame under the crucible of becoming so that such inward alchemy could take place.

Mysticism seems to rise during times of intense change and stress. Add the sufficiency of current shadows and the breakdown of all certainties, and we have the ingredients for the current universal pursuit of spiritual realities. We live in a time in which more and more history is happening faster and faster than we can make sense of it. The habits of millennia seem to vanish in a few months and the convictions of centuries are crashing down like the twin towers of the World Trade Center in New York on September 11, 2001. And yet, the deconstruction of traditional ways of being may invite the underlying Spirit of which we are a part to break through.

So how can we birth this miracle within ourselves? How can we foster our natural birthright of spiritual presence? For many years I have been a student of the varieties of spiritual experience, but for many more years than that I have been the student of dogs and cats. Bringing the two together has given me an insight into the nature of both that I otherwise would not have had. It has involved the necessary bridging of nature and spirit, instinct and intelligence, and, ultimately, the discovery that the animals have been there before us and have innate knowing of God, or the One Reality, which is the life and unfolding of the universe. I do not mean to suggest that animals follow the human version of the mystic path, but rather that they are so naturally a part of the One Reality that they restore us to something like our original condition, one in which we discover the steps and stages of the path that leads us back to who and what we really are.

Many have written of the mystic path and tracked its myriad adventures and planes of development. I have found Evelyn Underhill, writing early in the twentieth century, to be one of the finest guides to the experience. In her great work *Mysticism,* she presents the mystic path as a series of eight organic stages: awakening, purification, illumination, voices and visions, contemplation and introversion, ecstasy and rapture, the dark night of the soul, and union with the One Reality. In reflecting on these stages, I've discovered that more often than not it has been my animals, especially my dogs, rather than just my readings of the mystics who have provided some of my best understandings of the nature of each of these stages and their importance for life. Though the fit may be somewhat like the mythic Procrustean bed, where victims were either truncated or stretched to fit a preset form, the correlations have a genuineness if not a perfect accuracy. But before I launch into specific stories of dogs that that offer rough approximations with these stages, following is a brief summary of them as they are found in classical mysticism.

In the first stage, "awakening," one wakes up, to put it quite simply. Suddenly, the world is filled with splendor and glory, and one understands that one is a citizen in a much larger universe. One is filled with the awareness that one is a part of an enormous Life, in which everything is connected to everything else and it is very, very good.

The second stage of mystical development is called "purification." Here one rids oneself of those veils and obstructions of the ordinary unexamined life that keep one from the knowledge that one has gained from awakening. One is released from old ways of being and recovers one's higher innocence. In traditional mysticism it can take the form of a very intense pursuit of asceticism. It can also take other forms of trying to create purity and beauty in the world, as, for example, the path of Saint Francis of Assisi, who rebuilt a church as part of his purification, or Hildegard of Bingen, who planted a garden so that God's nose might be engaged.

The traditional third stage is called the path of "illumination": one is illumined in the light. The light of bliss—often experienced as actual light—literally pervades everything. One sees beauty and meaning and pattern everywhere, and yet one remains who one is and able to go about one's daily work. The stage of illumination is also one that many artists, actors, writers, visionaries, scientists, and creative people are blessed to access from time to time.

The fourth stage is called "voices and visions." One sees, hears, senses with more than five senses—an amplitude of reality including things one has never seen before, such as beings of different dimensions, angels, archetypes, numinous borderine persons, or figures from other times and realms. It is a state of revealing and interacting with a much larger reality—including those spiritual allies that lie within us and the unfolding of the unseen gifts that we all contain.

The fifth stage is what Underhill and others call "introversion," which includes entering the silence in prayer and contemplation. It is a turning to the inner life, wherein one employs some of the vast resources of spiritual technology to journey inward to meet and receive Reality in its fullness. It results in daily life as a spiritual exercise, bringing the inner and the outer life together in a new way.

The sixth stage is referred to as "ecstasy and rapture." Here the Divine Presence meets the prepared body, mind, emotions, and psyche of the mystic, which, cleared of the things that keep Reality at bay, now can ecstatically receive the One. It involves the art and science of happiness.

But, alas, after all this joy and rapture, the next stage, the seventh, is what is termed the "dark night of the soul," obeying the dictum that what goes up must come down. Suddenly the joy is gone, the Divine Lover is absent, God is hidden, and one is literally bereft of everything. Here one faces the remaining shadows of old forms and habits of the lesser self, preparing one to become more available to the final stage.

The eighth and last stage is called the "unitive life." Here one exists in the state of union with the One Reality all the time. One is both oneself and God. For those who enter this state, it seems as if nothing is impossible; indeed, everything becomes possible. They become world changers and world servers. They become powers for life, centers for energy, partners and guides for spiritual vitality in other human beings. They glow, and they set others glowing. They are force fields, and to be in their fields is to be set glowing. They are no longer human beings as we have known them. They are fields of being, for they have moved from Godseed to Godself.

In this book, we discover that these stages are not just for the mystic, but have their everyday equivalence in a form that is recognizable to everyone. All of us have had experiences of awakening to the beauty and wonder around us. And we have known the rigor of releasing old habits, and even the creativity and joy that come from new ways of being and thinking. We cannot avoid the depression and psychic flatland that accompany the dark night of the soul, and we may even have glimpsed or possibly experienced moments of transcendent union.

The essence of this path is reflected in the love and goodness of our animals. For love is the supreme quality that underlies all of these stages. It is through the experience and practice of love that we travel to the heart of God and realize how great is the gift of our human existence. In this, we find resonance with the life of Saint Francis of Assisi, who loved and honored animals as friends of his soul and who was often seen as followed by, carrying, or even wearing some bird or wolf or lamb or caterpillar as he made his caring way through the darkness of his times.

In loosely following these eight stages, I will be telling stories from my life with dogs, showing how the unfolding of the mystical path in its simpler, everyday form closely parallels many of the ways in which dogs guide us to the larger life. This path and our valiant animal companions help us make sense of our own wandering in the confusing spiritual landscape of our era and of the world's collective pilgrimage toward its next stage.

When harried by a life of too many commitments and deadlines, I always announce that in my next incarnation I plan to be a dog—the kind who lives an unscheduled life. Of course, it will have to be a "transitional" dog, one who can sneak into its owner's library when no one is looking and read a book, for example. Within this whimsy lies the mystery of the human-dog-divine connection. Our dogs can serve as guides to a life richer than our expectations, more astonishing than all our dreams. It is not inconsequential that the English language allows for the dyslexia of the spelling of the word *dog*: *God* spelled backward.

The Original
Dog Story

A long, long time ago in a country far away, a noble king who had reigned well and justly for many years, and who had lived to know a worthy successor, felt his life journey to be complete. Together with his beloved wife and brothers, the king left his great city, determined to climb the high holy mountain and enter Paradise while still in a human body. A kind and gentle dog joined them at the city gates and traveled with them.

During the long and arduous journey upward, the king's companions one by one fell away into the limitless abyss. Only the dog was left to keep him loving company. At last, aged and weary, the king, carrying the equally aged and footsore dog in his arms, reached the doorway to the realms of glory. The gatekeeper recognized him and welcomed him joyously.

"Your family and all your friends are inside, longing to greet you. Just set the dog down, and come in," the gatekeeper said. "He has no place within these doors."

"You mean this faithful dog is not allowed in Paradise?" the king asked, incredulous. "He's been with me all this way, and he loves me. How can I possibly leave him behind?"

"You must; you've given up everything else. It's not a cruelty to the dog; he simply does not belong in Paradise. Set him down and come in. Your family is so eager to embrace you. And the wind is icy out here."

"I won't come in without the dog," announced the king. "Paradise won't be paradise for me if the only way I get in is by abandoning an animal who has been good to me. Shut the gates. We'll stay out here together."

"Come in! Come in!" cried the gatekeeper. "You have been faithful to the end and so has your dog. Your dog is a living example of the dharma, the way of truth. He has been with you always. Come in. Come in."

And the great king and his dog entered Paradise.

MYSTICAL DOGS

Animals as Guides
to Our Inner Life

CHAPTER ONE

Chickie and the Path of Awakening

We were both pups when my parents got her—I about eighteen months old, she somewhat younger but older by far in wisdom and experience. She had already had a brief career in the movies, having played one of Daisy's puppies in the Dagwood and Blondie series. But now, too old for the part, she had been given to my father in lieu of payment for a script he had turned in. He was a comedy writer for radio and occasionally movies, and excelled in writing jokes and scripts but not in collecting the fees owed him.

Her name was Chickie, and she was a wonderful mix of Welsh corgi and bearded collie. A white star blazed on her chest, and she had four white feet and a white tipped tail to complement her long black fur. Even though she was scarcely over a year old, she was already motherly and sat by my crib for hours on end, making sure that no harm would come to me. If I cried, she would be off to my mother, insisting that she come immediately. If I wanted to play, she would bring toys, hers as well as mine.

My Dad caught on that this was a special dog with high intelligence plus something else. He taught her many tricks, learned

7

from the dog trainers at the movie studio. Lassie's trainers gave him pointers on how to get Chickie to respond to hand signals, as well as to climb ladders, bark on cue, walk on beach balls, dance on two legs, and jump rope with a willing human. This she did readily and well, but there was more to her still—perhaps one would call it a deep sense of ethics. She seemed virtue incarnate, a Saint Francis of Assisi of dogs, who took on responsibilities of saintly cast. I thought of her as my sister and, what with all of our travels, my constant and closest friend.

Thus it was a shock when one day one of the actors in a picture my father was working on came home with him, saw Chickie, and immediately wanted to buy her. "Jack," said the actor, "that is the greatest dog I ever saw in my life. I'll give you fifty bucks for that dog."

"Can't do it, pal," said my father. "It's the kid's dog."

The actor persisted. "I'll give you a hundred bucks for the dog. I know you need the money." Indeed, we did, and driven by the panic of incipient poverty, the one thing he dreaded more than any thing else, my father acted in an uncharacteristic manner.

Excusing himself, he went into the kitchen to discuss this with my mother. "Certainly not!" she adamantly declared. "It's Jeanie's dog."

"You're right, Mary," my father sheepishly agreed. "It's just that I think I'm going to lose my job at the studio and am damned scared of not being able to bring home the bacon."

"Well, you certainly cannot bring home the bacon by selling the child's dog," my mother fumed. "Anyway, if we go broke again, I'll just do what I always do—start an acting school for children."

A few days later the actor came back, saying, "Jack, I've got to have that dog on my ranch. I *want* that dog. I'll give you 250 bucks for the dog."

During this ordeal Chickie and I were sitting on the floor behind the couch, listening in horror. I was already making my running-away plans with her.

"Well, I sure do need the money," said my father. "Just a minute; I've got to talk to my wife."

"Mary, he's offering 250 bucks for the dog! We can always get Jeanie a new dog at the pound!"

"No way!" said my mother.

The next day the actor returned. He had rarely known failure and was not about to start now. "Jack, I'll give you 250 bucks and my secondhand car. I know you need a car to get around."

"Wait a minute," said my father. "I'm sure this time I can convince my wife."

Upon hearing the latest offer, my mother, bless her heart, stormed out of the kitchen, stalked up to the actor, and chewed him out. "Ronald Reagan," she railed, "how dare you try to take away my child's dog!"

At least he knew a good dog when he saw one.

Maybe it was that threat of being parted from each other, but after that incident with the actor, Chickie and I took to having long jaunts with each other. We would be gone for hours at a time, and either my parents were too busy to notice or they trusted Chickie's care of me. With Chickie in charge, I was given a great deal of freedom to wander in a world as miraculous as it was marvelous.

Behind our house was a large wooded area where Chickie and I began what I have come to think of as our travels in awakening. Two hours with Chickie in the woods yielded an incredible range of learnings. Chickie was more nose than eyes, and I quite the other way around. But together we investigated the endless treasures of forest and meadow. I remember crawling on four legs in order to follow more closely her interests and discoveries. As she sniffed out deer scat, mice holes, squirrel trails, and bug routes, she would occasionally turn around and check with me to see if I saw them too.

Chickie taught me to be alert to both the seen and the unseen, the heard and the unheard. A whisper of wings would turn her head and mine would follow, waiting for the flutter that would finally announce to my human-hindered head, "Bird on the wing!" Chickie would lift her nose, her tail would signal attention, and we would be off and running to follow the adventures of the air—entrancing molecules luring us to destinies both savory and dangerous. Once it was to a camper's discarded remnants of fried chicken, but once, too, it was to meet up with the snarling fury of a bobcat. Chickie barked, and I, knowing that human words were useless, barked too. Our defiant duet seemed to work, for the bemused cat slunk off, never to be seen again.

Chickie gave me metaphors for my later life's work, especially when it came to digging. Paws scratching away at apparently nothing soon revealed dark secrets hidden in the earth—old bones, ancient feathers, and things so mysterious as to be beyond human knowing. Years later I would probe and dig into the soil of the human subconscious with something like Chickie's fervor to find there the bones of old myths, the feathers of essence, and the great mysterious matrix that still sustains and lures the human quest.

Those early years with Chickie were a whole education in

looking, hearing, smelling, tasting, touching—the feast and lore of the senses. For many years now I have been helping schools in the United States and many other countries to improve education by making it sensory rich, hands on, art centered. When asked who my mentors have been—John Dewey? Maria Montesori? The Carnegie Institute?—I can only reply in truth, "Chickie."

Chickie and I traveled in others ways as well. In fact, we crossed the Mississippi river by train many times before I could spell it. "There it goes, Jeanie-pot!" my father would bleat with excitement. "There goes the Mississippi, the father of waters. Quick, look out your window while you can still see it."

"I've seen it," I'd say, my eye affixed firmly to my comic book.

"Whaddya mean, you've seen it? The greatest river in the world! The crossroads of American history—La Salle, Showboat, the Louisiana Purchase, Huckleberry Finn! And you say you've seen it."

"But Daddy, we just passed over it going the other way a couple of weeks ago."

"Yeah . . . well, that show in New York didn't pan out too well. We'll give California another try. I think I can get back with Bob Hope, and if not, Fibber McGee and Molly could always find room in their closet for me, and if not them, I could always try . . ." Two days later he was writing for Amos and Andy, and if he was lucky, we were set in one place for thirteen weeks—maybe.

For years Chickie served as the center for calm and a kind of spiritual tranquillity in our life of constant change brought about through my Dad's work as well as his penchant for eccentric adventures. Even though I went to something like twenty different schools all over the country before I was twelve, I would always come home to Chickie, who regarded all of life as delightful and

11

who maintained a saintly comportment and stability in the face of any whimsy we humans could invent.

People sometimes ask me how I can keep myself in reasonable mental and physical health even though I sometimes travel up to a quarter of a million miles a year and have a life of ridiculous complexity. In reflection I realize that Chickie's influence continues, to wit: Stay centered in eternity regardless of how much chaos is happening in time; look upon all people and events as opportunities for furthering life and its promise; and greet everyone as a potential awakened one—God in hiding, or dog in drag!

In addition to taking care of us Chickie also taught me my best lessons in ethics and responsibility. She seemed to have little self-interest. Many of her actions were clearly for others. She was empathy personified, whether in consoling with me when I was upset or in the way she would listen to humans as they railed against their supposed fate. Her answer was simply to be there, to place her head upon their knee and look at them sweetly in the eye, her gaze unblinking and never wavering. However, if their blue mood went on too long, she would try to entertain them, bringing over something to throw or, if that did not work, amusing them with one of her dancing tricks.

When my little brother was born, it was under Chickie's tutelage that I came to take care of him. I remember when he was very young, he managed to bang together some orange crates in the shape of a rocket. For weeks he had been telling us that he was going back home to where he came from up among the stars. One day, Chickie came madly running toward me, barking in distress and pulling me by my dress to our bedroom. I raced after her and found my little brother balancing in the open window in his "rocket." He waved happily at me saying, "Bye, bye. I go up home now." I grabbed his little body and pulled him back as the rocket fell eleven floors to the street.

Entering into another realm, that of the spiritual epiphany, Chickie accompanied me on the most important experience of my entire lifetime. It turned out to be my key experience in awakening. I have described it in other books, but not from the perspective of Chickie's critical role in it. It happened in my sixth year. I had been sent to Catholic school in Brooklyn, New York. My father had been tossed off the Bob Hope show for an excess of high spirits, and we were broke and living with my mother's Sicilian parents in the Italian section of that noble if bad-mouthed borough.

Theologically precocious, and buttressed with questions designed by my agnostic comedy-writing father, I would assail the little nun who taught our first grade with queries that seemed logical to me but blasphemous to her. "Sister Theresa, when Ezekiel saw the wheel, was he drunk?" Or "Sister Theresa, I counted my ribs and I counted Joey Mangiabella's ribs, and we have the same number of ribs, and so do all the other boys and girls. See? (At that moment, on cue, all the children in the class lifted up their undershirts to prove the point.) "So if God took a rib out of Adam to make Eve like you said, how come . . .?"

Then there were the Jesus questions. "Sister Theresa, how do you know that Jesus wasn't walking on rocks below the surface when he seemed to be walking on the water?" And "Sister Theresa, when Jesus rose, was that because God filled him full of helium?"

Then there was the day of the question that tipped her dogma as well as her dignity. It had to do with Jesus' natural functions and whether he ever had to go to the toilet. Her response had her looking like a black and white penguin in a state of hopping rage. She

13

jumped on a stool, tacked up a large sheet of heavy cardboard, and in large India-ink letters wrote:

JEAN HOUSTON'S YEARS IN PURGATORY

All further theological questions of an original bent met with the little nun X-ing in more years for me to endure in purgatory, and each X stood for a hundred thousand years! By the last day of the first grade I had accumulated something like 300 million years in purgatory to my credit. Spiritually bereft, I told my father about the debacle and he, finding it very funny, took me off immediately to see the motion picture *The Song of Bernadette*. This famous movie is renowned for its scenes of Saint Bernadette's vision of the holy Madonna in the grotto at Lourdes, which thereafter became a famous place for healing. Unfortunately, during the holiest of scenes, with Mother Mary appearing in luminous white in the grotto before the praying Bernadette, my father burst into long, whinnying, uncontrolled laughter. It turned out that he had known the starlet playing the role of Mary and found the incongruity between her Hollywood life and the role she was playing hilarious. Leaving the theatre finally in a state of mortal embarrassment, I pulled away from my still laughing father in order to get quickly to my house to emulate Bernadette's remarkable vision.

My destination was a guest room with a very long closet that looked a lot like a grotto. There were no clothes in the closet for Chickie had commandeered it as a nest for her new eight puppies. I explained my need to Chickie, feeling that she would not mind my moving her pups, being as she would want me to open a space for the greatest mama of them all to show up. When she protested mildly, I further explained that I didn't want the Holy Mother to

14

step on her pups. After that, Chickie watched my actions with interest.

Kneeling in the now cleared Brooklyn "grotto," I prayed to the Madonna to show up in the closet as she had for Bernadette at Lourdes. I began by closing my eyes and counting slowly to 10, while promising to give up candy for two weeks if she would only show up. I opened my eyes to encounter the Madonna Chickie lovingly carrying one of pups back into the "grotto." I kept on counting to ever higher numbers, promising all manner of food sacrifices—mostly my favorite Sicilian delicacies like chicken with lemon and garlic sauce—but my revelation was only to be more and more puppies back in the closet. Finally I counted to a very high number, 167, and having given up all calories, I told the Holy Mother that I could not think of anything else to give up, so would she *please, please, please* show up as I really wanted to see her. This time I was sure that she would make it. I opened my eyes, and there was Chickie contentedly licking all eight of her puppies.

"Oh Chickie," I sighed and reached out to pat her, whereupon she bestowed on me a kindly lick and a compassionate look as if I were her ninth puppy. At that moment came a vague spiritual forewarning, as if I had prayed for the Madonna and seen her in one of her many forms in Chickie, the all wise, all loving mother, and her care for her pups. But still I yearned for the movie version and did not yet recognize the truth of what I had been given. And so Herself offered me another chance. In a dreamy, unspecified state I went over to the window seat and looked over at the fig tree blooming in our yard. And suddenly it all happened—the most important awakening state of my entire life.

As I have written, "I must in my innocence have unwittingly tapped into the appropriate spiritual doorway, for suddenly the key turned and the door to the universe opened. Nothing changed in my outward perceptions. There were no visions, no sprays of golden light, certainly no appearance by the standard brand Madonna. The world remained as it had been. Yet everything around me, including myself, moved into meaning."[1]

Only in reflection have I come to realize how much of what I then felt and knew had been prepared for me by Chickie and her guidance in the ways of awakening. All those rambles that we had taken together were now one ramble, all the smells and sights of nature to which she had introduced me were present along with the fig tree blooming in the yard, Chickie herself and her pups in the closet, the plane in the sky, the sky itself, and even my idea of the Madonna. All had become part of a single unity, a glorious symphonic resonance in which every part of the universe was a part of and illuminated every other part, and I knew that in some way it all worked together and it was very good.

My mind had awakened to a consciousness that spanned centuries and was on intimate terms with the universe. Just as Chickie had taught me, everything was interesting and important: deer scat, old leaves, spilled milk, my Mary Jane shoes, the fig tree, the smell of glue on the back of the gold paper stars I had just pasted on the wall paper, the stars themselves, my grandfather Prospero Todaro's huge stomach, the Atcheson, Topeka, and Santa Fe railroad, Uncle Henry (the black porter who took care of me on the train across the country), the little boy fishing in the lake who waved to me on the train when I was crossing Kansas, the chipped paint on the ceiling, my nana's special stuffed artichokes, my father's typewriter, the silky ears of corn in a Texas cornfield, my Dick and Jane reader, and all the music that ever was—all were in a state of resonance and of the most immense and ecstatic kinship.

I was in a universe of friendship and fellow feeling, a companionable universe filled with interwoven Presence and the dance of life. This state seemed to go on forever, but it was actually only about two seconds, for the plane had moved only slightly across the sky. I had entered into timelessness, the domain in which eternity was the only reality and a few seconds could seem like forever.

Somewhere downstairs I heard the door slam, and my father entered the house laughing. Instantly, the whole universe joined in. Great roars of hilarity sounded from sun to sun. Field mice tittered, and so did angels and rainbows. Even Chickie seemed to be chuckling. Laughter leavened every atom and every star until I saw a universe inspirited and spiraled by joy, not unlike the one I read of years later in the *Divine Comedy* when Dante described his great vision in paradise: "*D'el Riso d'el Universo*" (the joy that spins the universe). This was a knowledge of the way everything worked. It worked through love and joy and the utter interpenetration and union of everything with the All That Is. And the Madonna—Chickie—was at the center of it all.

In this direct knowledge lay what I later learned was the mystical experience. This experience is not something to be kept sacrosanct in esoteric cupboards. It is coded into our bodies, brimming in our minds, and knocking on the doors of our souls. It is our natural birthright, and naturally it is most available when we are still children. As a child it charged me and changed me and probably gave me the impetus to do the things I later did. It showed me the many faces of God, and for weeks afterward I went around seeing this face in every creature, plant, and person—even in Sister Theresa, who was somewhat bothered by my beaming approval of her inner self.

"Madonna, Madonna, show up, show up!" I had shouted.

And of course the Madonna had showed up, present in Chickie with her unconditional love and care for her pups and for me. Kneeling in front of her and her altar of puppies, I had asked for everything and *everything* is just what I got. And even today, whenever I see a statue of Mary I can not help but be reminded of Chickie's boundless love, the ultimate Madonna bringing the puppies back into the closet, bringing them back into the manger.

As it happened, Chickie lived for a very long time (something like 140 years of dog time), suffering little but one very original and mystical neurosis. As soon as she boarded a train and for about an hour or two afterward, she got the stigmata: all four paws would begin to bleed like the hands and feet of some medieval saint. The vet could never figure out why this would happen, so we all accepted my mother's Catholic interpretation of it as being a sign of God's favor. Certainly, by her actions and saintly comportment, Chickie belonged among the circle of the blessed, so it seemed very reasonable that, along with Saint Francis of Assisi, she should be so honored.

Chickie lived with us until around my ninth year. Then one day, my father took her by the leash and told me to say good-bye to her at the elevator door of our apartment building. He informed me that he was going to give her to a friend who had a farm in Connecticut.

"Why, Daddy? Why would you give her away? She's my sister. You can't just go and give away my sister and best friend!"

"You kids are not taking her out for walks enough, and she will be happier on the farm."

And with that my dear Chickie left my life forever. To this day I have never understood why my father took her away. In retrospect, however, I realize that at that time he was starting to leave us in order to marry another, and perhaps getting rid of Chickie was one of his first acts of detachment.

When I was seventeen, my mother rented a summer house for us on Green Farms Road near Westport, Connecticut. Daily, my brother and I would take long bike rides along Green Farms Road. I always felt that somewhere on that road was something that I had lost, and if only I could find it, I would be restored to grace again.

Several times that summer my father came up to visit us. After each visit, he'd leave to "visit a friend who has a farm further up on Green Farms Road." Just before my Dad died in 1986 he told me that he also had been visiting Chickie, who even at that time was living very happily on that farm. He never told me that she was just up the road, but something in my soul must have known she was there, since I felt so called to journey up and down that road on my bike. That she was very happy on the farm I have no doubt for she lived to be more than twenty years old.

Chickie was only the first of the remarkable dogs I have known and loved who have revealed to me, through their oneness with nature, facets of the mystical path. Unsullied in their essence and with a natural attunement to the Source, they have a purity that makes them wonderful companions as well as guides for our path back to wholeness.

Chickie was the means for me to understand on the most primal levels the nature of "awakening," the initial stage on the mystical journey. Under her innocent tutelage, I experienced that place where the field of our being shifts and the deepest coding of our life emerges, an unlooked for act of grace. In her presence something in me woke up, rising through all my parts and seeming to reconstitute the whole. My senses became more acute, gaining something that our animals just naturally experience—the air flooded with information, the land infinitely interesting and full of continuous surprises to engage the eye, enthrall the nose, astonish the ear. All flowers become friends, humble bread tastes of manna from heaven, and every thing and every one seem lit from within—a kingdom of God in the midst of what we once thought of as ordinary reality.

Long after Chickie was gone, I found words to describe the experiences I had shared with her in the poetic succinctness of poet and mystic William Blake: "To see a World in a grain of Sand, / And a Heaven in a Wild Flower, / Hold Infinity in the palm of your Hand, / And Eternity in an Hour."[2] Blake also said, "If the doors of perception were cleansed, / Everything would appear as it is, Infinite . . ."[3]

Awakening can have the most tremendous effect for good on the lives of those who experience it, as it had on me after my own revelation, making them wonderfully creative and useful. They seem to live at a higher level, with insight and ideas from some larger expanse of mind, to the betterment of their fellows and community. Yet few arbiters of reality recognize the place where these awakened ones dwell, or dare name it. Whether awakening begins in surprise as a gift from God or from grace or from evolution or from a peculiar synchronicity between nature's elements and one's own state of receptivity or from a wonderful dog, one feels powerfully affected by the sheer unexpected glory of it all.

What we think of as nature mysticism often occurs with such surprise. You are watching the ocean come in, and suddenly you are on every shore, in every ocean, and within every shining drop. And why not? If we are part of the One Reality, as mystics tell us

20

and as many physicists confirm, we are ubiquitous through this universe and in touch with all its parts and particulars. It just takes the shift in consciousness that awakening awakens to experience this absolutely.

In my childhood, Chickie was my William Blake, providing by her own being the key to an experience that showed me that everything was interrelated in an organic universe founded on truth and beauty and a pattern that connected everything with everything else. Early on, I was able to see that all this was part of a holy perfection and was utterly serving of the good. With Chickie as spiritual guide, I also experienced timelessness and entered that state in which the categories of time are strained by the tensions of eternity. I came to realize that what we call normal time is just the veneer of infinite time. Great eternity surrounds us and indwells us, and we come to think of past, present, and future as merely special laws within its much larger laws. I discovered then that we are citizens in a much larger universe and that we are able to enter into this kingdom of the larger order here and now.

In its everyday form, awakening is experienced as mindfulness—being present and awake to the sights and sounds and particulars of our daily lives. We go off of robot and become alert to the splendor of existence, be it seen in a sunset or a rose, an old man's craggy face, the eyes of an animal, or the side of a mountain. We become awake to the nuances of emotion that pass between ourselves and others. And we respond in turn with a fuller expression to the other's need or question. We move beyond that half-asleep state called ordinary waking consciousness.

And when we do, reality changes. We find ourselves in a world so startling in its vividness, so alive and resplendent in all its parts that we wonder at what planet we have arrived. We realize that we have lived as dim and diminished versions of ourselves, and vow to do so no longer. Chickie was my conduit to this larger reality. With her guidance I came awake to a world once known, long forgotten but held in trust by dogs for their human charges should they agree to follow their lead.

However it comes, awakening is the greatest experience of remembering who and what we really are, why we are here, and how it all fits together. Waking up has never been more important than at the beginning of the new millennium because, as of this moment, the species we call human is on a collision course with global cataclysm. Awakening brings with it answers, solutions, new ways of seeing and doing and being, and, best of all, the impetus to follow through and bring these answers into our particular world and time. Solutions to our current dilemmas are coded in what we might call symbolically the Mind of the Maker, the Warehouse of God. In states of consciousness such as those awakening stimulates, the bandwidth increases and, with it, the capacity to access this greater realm of knowledge and creativity.

Strange as it seems, we can do this. Judging from the accounts of so many who have had an awakening experience, such access is always there—it is part of our innate human equipment. These experiences are fundamental to the human condition; they are part of our inheritance, the deeper givens of our existence. They are probably coded into our mind/brain system and are our call back to our "spiritual home place."

The opportunity for us today is how to take this natural ability and make it normal, an ordinary-extraordinary part of our regular experience. How can we engage in everyday applied awakening? The story of Chickie gives us some important clues. Chickie was ever curious, always looking, sniffing, digging, and rolling in the continuous revelation of nature, discovering its sumptuous wonders and sharing them with me. For us this means to go forth and do likewise. It means that we halt our automatic responses to things, cease living a posthumous existence.

One celebrated way of doing this is the "stop" or "gathering mindfulness" technique, in which one is able to wake up to the realities both within oneself and without. To begin, walk around the room, but then take a few seconds to stop and become conscious of everything you are doing, seeing, hearing, and feeling—in other words, allowing the moment to become charged with presence. Suddenly the world ceases to be just background noises and becomes a richness, and your brain/mind system ceases to be on automatic as you reorganize your perceptions into mindfulness.

Do this "stop" exercise now for the next few minutes—simple things like picking up a glass, walking to the door, looking at your shoes. But stop before you take any action, and then do the same action or act of attention consciously, bringing full mindfulness into the act. As you become more conscious of your actions, you will become more naturally aware and alert. Your field of mindfulness will expand and you will feel yourself inhabiting your reality and not just being a bystander.

If you would start by practicing this technique for five minutes a day, then gradually increasing day by day the minutes in which you stop before performing any movement and then doing it mindfully, in a month's time you will be well on your way to having gone off of automatic and into conscious orchestration of your life. Your senses will have expanded because, together with your continuing to journey and explore in imagination your inner sensory world, you will have done much to reweave your perceptions. And not just your perceptions. This simple technique will spill over into your relationships, memory, thinking, and feeling, as well as increasing your capacity to learn and even to create.

Life, then, is no longer a dream but a vast creative enterprise in which one can focus one's enhanced energies and attention to partner with creation itself. Too many people go through life oblivious to most of what is around them, several times removed from reality and many times removed from any passion for the possible. Mindfulness gives passion with clarity. Most spiritual traditions consider it to be the best possible state of being. With regard to the outer world, it is a quality of heightened awareness and awakeness to life and its experiences. It can be described as becoming alert for 360 degrees. With regard to the inner world, mindfulness demands similar awareness, so that you become able to orchestrate your internal states, whether it be for creative exploration in inner realms or for meditation and prayer.

There is also the state of mindfulness that is referred to as "being conscious of being conscious," what the mystic philosopher and consciousness teacher G. I. Gurdjieff referred to as "self-remembering." In this state you are aware of yourself reading my words, but you are also aware of the experiences you have just explored in the last few minutes as well as the background of sensations in the room where you are sitting, your own bodily sensations, ideas that cross your mind, and your general mood— all of these held together simultaneously. You are aware of all these things, but on the front burner of your consciousness you are also aware that you are aware. I know I am asking much of you, but isn't your life worth it?

To further awakening, devote time to explore and celebrate beauty in nature as well as in poetry, art, music, and the emerging spirit of the times, with its budding of new realities in the wake of the winter of a passing age. Gather unto yourself congenial friends—two-legged as well as four-legged—who share your drive toward awakening so that you keep on advancing on the path.

Immersion in beauty wherever you find it calls forth inner beauties and brings to consciousness the freshness of a world made new. Reading the rich metaphors of poetry especially can shake the mind from its stolid moorings, and you see deeper into the world and time. Perception becomes more acute, and conception as well. You wake up to what is going on around you, become empathic, know yourself as part of a seamless kinship with all living things. Thus you come to feel and care more deeply about the decay and degradation in the social and moral order. Like Chickie, you become sensitive to other people's pain as well as joy and offer them the companionship of soul. You reverence their being and hold them as holy—gods in hiding. This helps them to awaken as well as keeping the spirit of possibility alive in yourself.

You say "Yes!" to life wherever you find it, abandon whining, and welcome and celebrate the springtide of change. Like a happy dog, greet each day with wonder and astonishment. Then grace happens, shift happens, and the mind is prepared to receive Reality in all its many colors and textures.

Awakening further requires that you take time and space out of your usual day for a practice of spiritual connection. We know that the universe is a living system of elegant design that seems intent on providing the opportunity for learning on all levels. Access levels of consciousness on the divine wavelength, and the learning unfolds. We are built to travel the wavelength of consciousness and to enlarge it when we wish to live in a larger universe.

Better still, change perspective through meditation, reflection, or focus, and discover yourself to be the latest flower on the tree of the cosmos, ready to bloom. This requires the sun and rain of attention, a conscious dwelling in the midst of eternal fecundity. What had been there dimly as background awareness then moves to the foreground. In this state anything that you concentrate on opens up—objects, ideas, relationships, business, governance, even grand designs. We awaken to the wealth of being and the "Aha!" experiences keep on coming.

Above all, let your animals guide you. They know the way.

CHAPTER TWO

Champ and the Journey of Release

Long snout, eyes alert and waiting for you to move and make things happen. A constant look of "What's next?" Tail poised in readiness, revealing an attitude of "Let's go for it!" That was my smooth-haired fox terrier, Champ. He was a beauty—a sleek white body mixed with brown and black patterns; a mostly black face, interrupted by elegant brown arching eyebrows; sophisticated tan etchings along his jawline, as if God's own cosmetician had worked him up. His specialty was the utter joy of living. Never have I known any creature—two-legged, four-legged, finned or feathered—who exulted so hugely in the sheer gladness of being alive.

Champ greeted each morning with a whoop of doggie joy, dancing his celebration of awakening. This took at least five minutes, a prancing ritual performance that assured everyone that life was so very good. When I returned from school or an outing, as soon as I pushed open the door I had to drop my school books or whatever else I was carrying because he would leap into my arms, greeting me as if I were the long-lost love of his life. "I am so *happy, happy, happy* to see you!" he seemed to say. And this occurred all the time, every day, from the moment we got him at four months old when I was in early adolescence until the day he died fourteen years later.

While Chickie had accompanied me through my childhood learnings, Champ, my next dog, was a marvelous companion for the sorrows of adolescence. He would listen intently, his head cocking from side to side as I rambled on about my sickness of heart: my parents separating and divorcing, my being kicked out of Performing Arts High School for "lack of talent." One year, I told him about how nobody invited me to the senior prom even though I was president of the student body of Julia Richman High School. As president I was required to attend the prom, and my young aunt had to get her girlfriend's twenty-nine-year-old brother, a pharmacist, to take me to the prom. After bouts of teenage angst I held long conversations with Champ, wondering whether life was worth living. "Give me an answer, Champ. Talk to me, please," I'd cajole.

In answer, Champ would climb into my lap and cover my face with kisses. I realize now that I probably spoke more to him than to any other friend or relative. He was the receiver of all my secrets, the one who held my soul in confidence. But, then, for millennia dog ears have been the receptacle for the human heart. One thinks of the cave man Gog, some one hundred and fifty centuries ago, bemoaning with his wolf by the fire the wooly mastodon that got away. Or, more currently, a reigning queen whispering to her corgis about the marital problems of her children.

With Champ I grew up. He accompanied me and witnessed my progress from ninth grade through graduate school and beyond, as I began my career as a college professor and researcher into human capacities. With Champ lying by my feet as I studied and thought and wrote, I planted the major seeds of my mind. To this day I cannot read Greek philosophy without hearing a phantom *thump, thump, thump* of the merry tail that had accompanied my pursuit of Plato. Champ saw me grow from an angular child into a woman's body and was the most physically present of any being I had ever known. In fact, for the better part of his life we were sleeping back-to-back on the same narrow bed, leaving me spinally tapped into terrier reality. Maybe that's what led to my ability to communicate with dogs and also to Champ's accurate assessment as to where to lead me next. We had caught each other's soul force, had become spiritually resonant with each other in our long years of backbone connectedness.

He would generally wake up earlier than I and begin his ritual of sitting up and watching my face for any slight sign of waking up. He always seemed to know whether I was really asleep or just faking it. Then his forbearance would vanish, and he would begin his doggy dance up and down the whole course of my body, ending in a frantic licking of my face. "Get up now!" he would be saying. "Life is short, and we've got miles to go and things to do!"

Throughout the fourteen years of *his* life he accompanied me through the major rituals of *my* life, as I left behind one body for another, childhood for adolescence, and adolescence for maturity— divesting myself from one form of existence for another. He was my releaser from old ways of being, my purifier who helped prepare me for new stages. What was strange and mysterious about this merry little dog was that whenever I would moan about some great question in my life—"What's it all about?" or "Is there anybody out there?"—Champ would grab his leash in his mouth and urge me to go out with him.

Attached to the leash in good umbilical fashion, I would often let him lead me on the walk. Frequently he would follow a

29

favored path, from Park Avenue down 86th Street to Fifth Avenue and into Central Park to play with his many dog friends. But sometimes he would not. And it was then that the mystery would occur and he would pull me in another direction, one that would initiate a new stage in my personal development. On several occasions this would have to do with our meeting a significant person, whose presence would subtly—or not so subtly—shift the course of my life. Champ had an especial penchant for discovering wise old men, two of whom I would like to acknowledge here.

Very early in life, I had become enamored of ancient Greek art. I would regularly visit the nearby Metropolitan Museum of Art to wander through the rooms containing the statues and artifacts of ancient Greece. The cool gaze of the marble gods and their archaic smiles affected me with the shock of meeting long known and much beloved friends. The reproduction of the Parthenon of Athens filled me with longing for something that lay beyond memory, beyond words. Amidst those friezes and sculptures I felt that I had come home from a very long journey.

Thus it was serendipitous when one day Champ changed his ordinary beeline to Central Park and tugged me instead along Madison Avenue, where I chanced upon a shop that had a beautiful fourth-century B.C. frieze of the goddesses Demeter and Persephone in the window. The shop's owner, Dr. Biedermeir, was a well-known antiquarian and had sold antiquities to Sigmund Freud before he escaped from Vienna in the wake of Hitler's persecution of Jewish people. After that first day, I would stare regularly in the window, wishing I had the money to buy this magnificent piece, but it cost $200! (Nowadays, it would be more like $20,000.) Then one day a schoolteacher bought it and it was gone from the window when we arrived.

As I sadly moved away from the shop, Champ pulled me back. Standing in the doorway was Dr. Biedermeir, gesturing for Champ and me to enter his store. He told me that he was much taken with my look of longing in the window and was wondering if perhaps he should teach me how to appreciate, date, and repair antiquities. "I need a student, *ja*? And you love these ancient things, no?"

"Oh yes—yes sir," I replied, and Champ wagged his tail in agreement.

"Then you and your little dog will come some times and I will teach you something of my craft," he invited.

And with that my training began. I look back and can see myself handling antiquities with extreme care, learning how to date bronze statues of Hermes, Athena, and, once, a greyhoundlike dog of the second century B.C. "Look Champ," I exclaimed, holding the bronze dog out to him, "your great-great-great-great-grandma." Champ sniffed curiously at his ancient ancestress, but then went back to the chew bone Dr. Biedermeir had so kindly provided him. From these beginnings began my avocation as a part-time archaeologist as well as a collector of antiquities. As I was writing this chapter, my dogs Luna and Zeus would lounge amidst Greek and Roman statues, an Egyptian sarcophagus, and even a four-thousand-year-old wooden Anubis, the god-dog-jackal of ancient Egypt who led the souls into the afterlife.

Champ also led me to another elderly gentleman and what was to become one of the most important friendships of my entire life. At fourteen, one day I ran into and knocked down an old man with a French accent while running down Park Avenue late for school. I'd taken to running a lot because of grief over my parent's divorce and the fact that I was now seeing less and less of

31

my much loved father since he had remarried. Up until that time, in whimsical fashion, we had been known as the "Jean and Jack show," being a father-daughter team in spontaneous and sometimes well-rehearsed performance art. Life with Dad had been a comedy team, filled with pratfalls, old stunts, and a huge amount of fun. I'd always considered myself enormously lucky in the father category compared with the stick-in-the-muds most of the other kids called "Dad." But now all of this was to be left behind, as my father rightly devoted his time and attention to his new marriage. I belonged to an earlier era in his life, and clearly I had to release my grief and regret at this changing form of my life. . . . Champ must have known this on some level, for he guided me to someone who could help fill the void in paternal companionship I now felt.

The elderly man I had crashed into and knocked down had bid me "*Bon voyage*" after I had picked him up and dusted him off, and I never expected to see him again. A week later, however, Champ took me through an unaccustomed route, down Park Avenue and away from the park. It was there on 84th Street that I was hailed by the same old man, who immediately expressed considerable delight on seeing Champ, telling us that he had known and loved an English fox terrier in his boyhood. We discussed the unique genius of the breed, and he agreed that they were "*sans doute* the smartest dog in the world." Champ's head cocked with interest at the man's French accent, I imagine because he had so carefully trained himself to understand American English. It was then that Champ, the man, and I began our long walks together on many Tuesdays and Thursdays. I have written of these walks in several of my other books, referring to the episodes as "Walking the dog with Mr. Tayer."

"Mr. Tayer" turned out to be the great French scientist, mystic, priest, and paleontologist Pierre Teilhard de Chardin. Up to now I have told only the human side of the story—how Teilhard showed me how, when sniffing the air, to be aware that molecules of everyone who had ever lived would be passing through me every few weeks; how clouds were God's calligraphy in the sky; and how a simple caterpillar on the grass was the Divine preparing itself for emergence into a butterfly and how I in my gawky adolescence was not unlike that mysterious caterpillar, preparing for the butterfly I would become. And most of all, how we were so fortunate to live in the most important time in history, when the peoples of Earth would be converging in what he called a "noosphere," a field of interlinked minds and cultures within which our possibilities would unfold at a tremendous rate, and, as a result, a new world would be born. Within this context, Teilhard always spoke of our need for purifying ourselves from styles and beliefs that were keeping us from the full revelation of spirit's intention for us.

Champ was very much a part of our conversations and an intricate component of our friendship. Occasionally Teilhard would look down at my dog and ask, "What do you think, Champ?" Or even, "Is that not so, Champ, *hein*?" To these inquiries Champ would wag his tale in assent, or when thoughts of special import were disclosed, he would stand on his hind legs and place his paws on Teilhard's knees.

Once we went to the Central Park zoo together. As we visited the amphibians and reptiles, the bears, lions, and monkeys, Teilhard showed me how evolution had progressed both in vertebrate structure and in the capacity to encompass richer activities, greater mental facility. As we passed the various cages and enclosures, he traced the metamorphosis of these creatures from one stage to another.

Finally, he stopped in front of a baby carriage and peered in. Champ rose on his hind legs and did the same, being a confirmed pram peeker.

"The next part of the evolutionary journey!" Teilhard proclaimed joyously. "This little baby contains all the stages we have seen in this zoo, and yet is so much more. She is part of a cosmic evolutionary movement that inspires us to unite with God. She includes and transcends all previous forms of development."

"But what about the trees and the rocks and the animals?" I asked, worriedly looking at Champ. "Aren't they important anymore? And what about Champ? I don't think I want to be part of this evolution stuff if Champ is left behind. Champ is a much better person than a lot of people I know! Does God forget all about him just because he's a dog and can't talk philosophy?"

Teilhard laughed and answered that Champ and the other animals were as important as ever but were now incorporated into and crowned by the noosphere. They and we were all part of a cosmic evolutionary movement that was moving us toward metamorphosis into a whole new form. As this metamorphosis continued, we would leave our littleness behind. I replied that I did not find any littleness in Champ—quite the contrary! Teilhard smiled and agreed that I was probably right.

Champ was curiously prescient about Teilhard's physical condition. For example, when I just thought he looked a little pale, Champ would press his nose into the old man's legs and look up at him meaningfully and with a worried expression. Indeed, the last time I ever saw Teilhard, Champ refused to leave, dragging along after me on the leash, whimpering while he looked back at his departing form. Teilhard and I had agreed to meet on the following Tuesday afternoon, and when I arrived at our accustomed spot,

Champ, usually merry, sank down in a state of dog depression, occasionally looking sadly up at me. I continued to keep our Tuesday and Thursday appointments for more than a month, always with the same unhappy reaction from Champ. It was only later that I learned that Teilhard had died and understood that Champ, with his doggy brand of omniscience, had known it.

My walks with Teilhard inspired me with intellectual passion, new directions for thought and feeling—not only seeing the divine in nature, but the action of spiritual intelligence in the history of Earth and the unfolding of higher forms of species through time. During these amblings, I was slowly released from my sorrows over leaving an important part of my past with my father. What came instead was joy in the journey of understanding the evolution of the universe and the metamorphosis from the simplest creatures to the universal human. Teilhard gave me a path to follow that in many ways, in spite of diverse and sundry side trips, I have never really left. I realize now that these walks with Champ and "Mr. Tayer" laid the literal groundwork for what was to become my search for those innate divine potentials in our human condition that help us to release ourselves from the killing fields of archaic history and action. Since walking with Champ and Teilhard, I have been dedicated to helping envision a higher future history and a new way of being human.

Champ continued to accompany me on many of my own journeys. Most summers my brother, Champ, and I were together in different parts of the country, either with relatives in Texas and Florida, or in summer houses my mother rented in New England and upstate New York. Wherever we went, Champ, an alpha dog if ever there was one, met the local dogs and often became their leader, regardless of the fact that he was frequently much smaller than they. He had a kind of dog charisma that appeared to enchant and engage all the other local dogs.

Fascinated by this talent and wanting to find out how he did it, I took to following him as he moved into a new summer neighborhood. He would walk down a street, meet a new dog, and, after their ritual sniffing, wag his tail madly and indicate with a bright jerk of his head that the dog should join him. He would do the same with the next dog they met, and before long he had acquired himself a pack. Together they would roam the area, playing madcap games or investigating new haunts and old smells. This would go on all summer, but if I happened to walk by and called him, he would give a brief bark to his compatriots as if to say, "Gotta go, pals. Herself needs me." The other dogs would give me gloomy looks and drop their tails as their "champion" departed.

Champ was with me on another kind of journey as well— my momentous transition from single to married status. My husband-to-be courted both of us, taking us on long walks in the forests and along the lakes of Connecticut and New York state. After we married, Champ remained a walking companion, living with my mother and brother just down the block from where we had set up housekeeping. As he was an essential member of my family's household, they were not about to release him into my new apartment. But Bob and I continued to take Champ on daily long walks, although he'd look wistful when I'd leave him off with my brother and mother.

I think of Champ as the "dog who took me places." He was present through the most important of my life changes, as I sorrowed over leaving old habits and thrilled over discovering the joys of new ones. Without his sympathy, I would have often been mired in a slough of despondency. (No doubt about it, dogs are antidepressants on four legs.) Without his vibrant company, I doubt that I would have met the crucial people I did or followed his lead into new paths. With his genius for acquiring a pack, he taught me the ways of networking and creating community, a skill that has proved very valuable in my work of setting up communities of co-learners all over the planet who can work together empowering each other to create a better world.

My life and learnings with Champ have a correlation with the stage in mystical development that follows awakening, which is known as "release and purification." Herein, we rid ourselves of old ways of being as well as those veils and obstructions of the ordinary unexamined life that keep us from using the knowledge gained from awakening. In awakening, we come to the recognition of the larger life in each of us. But there is still the stockpile of old habits to deal with. We are like flypaper, reluctant to give up the debris caught in the neural loops and emotional planes of our being. The process then is one of honing and refining so as to release the habits and patterns that keep us forgetful of our true state, thus allowing us to move to other stages in our evolution. With Champ by my side, I was led cheerfully along the path of release from childhood attitudes and adolescent sorrows to larger visions, broader scope.

As so many people on the mystic path have noted, when we try to get back to our experience of awakening, the old self sets ingenious traps to trick us and make us impotent before our higher calling. In this we have noble company, though it is cold comfort. Saint Paul, for one, complains, "For the good I would, I do not; but the evil which I would not, that I do." Paul then goes on to explain the deeper nature of this universal predicament, good psychologist that he was: "For I delight in the law of God after the inward man: But I see another law in my members, warring against the law of my mind, and bringing me into captivity to the law of sin which is in my members. O wretched man that I am! Who shall deliver me from the body of this death?" (Romans 7:22–24).

To place this scriptural rant in modern terms, we might say that we are amphibious beings dwelling in several worlds, not the least of which are the very primitive ones contained in older portions of our brains—the old reptilian and limbic systems—with all their built-in survival mechanisms and fortresses against ancient anxieties. Although protective of our well-being and critical to our survival, they keep us in outmoded attitudes and sabotage the yearnings of our higher brain functions. Two codings seem to be warring within us: habit and conditionings, and spiritual realization. The habit patterns being very deep, the ways of riddance have often been very radical; thus the extravagant efforts made in many mystical paths to release body, mind, and consciousness from the accumulations of one's own history so that one can be scrubbed so clean as to become available to transcendent new life. The senses have to be put into the service of a larger possibility; the soul and intellect have to be able to abandon all preconceptions and thoughts that keep them fixated on anything less than the wholeness and holiness of Reality.

To pursue this path of release and purification, seekers both East and West have engaged in the most strenuous behaviors— eating very little, sleeping not at all, wearing hair shirts, lying on nails. Whatever extremes of self-mortification the human mind can imagine, these have been done. The story of the Buddha is one of the most intriguing of all such accounts.

As a purification rite in his quest for enlightenment,

Siddhartha Gautama undertook for five years incredibly rigid self-discipline of the body. As he himself said, he sat with set teeth and tongue pressed against his palate, seeking "by sheer force of mind" to "restrain, coerce, and dominate" his heart until the "sweat streamed" from his armpits. He practiced holding his breath until he heard a roaring in his head and felt as if a sword were boring into his skull. He lived for periods on all sorts of nauseating foods, dressed in garments that gave him pain, stood for days in one posture, and moved or walked for months only in a squatting position. He sat on a couch of thorns, lay in the cemetery on charred bones among rotting corpses, let dirt and filth accumulate on his body till it dropped off of itself, and of course, inevitably, ate his own excrement. In the end, he reduced his diet to a single grain of rice or one jujube fruit a day. If he sought to feel his belly, it was his backbone that he found in his grasp.

You would think that all this would have brought results, but to Siddhartha's great distress, enlightenment was as far away as ever. "With all these severe austerities," he mused as he lay at death's door, "I fail to transcend ordinary human limits and rise to the heights of noblest understanding and vision. Could there be another path to enlightenment?"[1]

With this thought, he had himself rolled into the shallow water of a stream. Refreshed, he realized that the human body was the one instrument that human beings could use to attain enlightenment. Why, then, was he subjecting his physical instrument to such extreme self-mortification? In this moment of insight, he decided to return to a more natural life. His first symbolic act was to accept a bowl of curds from a village maiden, brought to him on the day of the full moon in the month of May. Thus strengthened, he sat in meditation under the famed bodhi tree until his goal of enlightenment was achieved.

Now, Buddha's example of purification is on the most extreme end of the spectrum. My releases with Champ as companion were of a more gentle nature, though nonetheless very painful for me. He modeled for me the releasing of the old and the embracing of the new through his exuberant attitude of "What's next?" Regardless of what might have happened the day before, he was ready every morning for new adventures that might take us to our next stage of development. At my strongest moments of emotional suffering, he would appear, leash in mouth, offering the lure of enticing possibilities that I could not resist.

Champ's innocent, open, utterly joyful way of greeting life is more a model for us, I believe, than some of today's current semipurifying practices. I sometimes wonder, for instance, whether some athletes are not misplaced mystics seeking purification through extreme forms of molding and muscling their bodies. Then there are the odd diets, the brutal exercise schedules, wheat grass, colonics, the steam and soak and wrap and purge regimes of the health spa, and other modern mortifications of the flesh. All these arise from the same exaggerated impulse of wanting to change past patterns. Of course, they do not turn one into a Buddha, but then neither did Siddhartha's ascetic practices.

We may be repulsed at the ways in which these ancient and modern ascetics attempt to purify and change themselves, and yet in a strange way do we not do the same? How many of us daily dwell on that which is repugnant, stretching ourself on the rack with a constant recall of painful thoughts and memories until much of our mind is eaten away with grief or terror? There is something in the human temperament that seems to demand a calling up of a dark consciousness by which we enter through the black hole of the universe and pass into another level of ourself. Some of those physical torments that the old saints put on themselves were child's play compared to some of the automatic and habitual mental tortures and chronic self-naughting we inflict upon ourselves. In this, we pathologize rather than mythologize. Perhaps it is because we have lost the sense of where we may yet go and what we truly are— Godseeds planted in plenty of manure so that we may grow into what we were originally intended to be.

There is, of course, a more positive way of viewing our need for purification and release from our old ways of being, which Sufi mystic Jalaluddin Rumi described as a path of "conscious suffering." Seen rightly, Rumi said, the cleansing and transforming power of suffering abides not in the degree of pain experienced, but in the degree of *acceptance achieved.* When one meets the action of God or Spirit in and through painful events, the soul is refined and deepened. Just as the beautiful ruby comes from the rock being crushed for millions of years, fine leather from the harshness of tanning, and fine wine from the crushing and fermentation of the grapes, so we might regard the sufferings of our life as refinements that are tanning us, fermenting us, transforming and deepening us. Brought into consciousness with acceptance rather than resentment, the ill treatment that we suffer at our own and others' hands is transformed into divine pressure that is molding and shaping the Godself within.

Such conscious acceptance of the process purifies our suffering and transmutes it into grace. You, the reader, might wish to think along these lines: "If I had not suffered, I would not have been able to . . . have compassion for others . . . gain in wisdom . . . take on tasks and challenges that seemed impossible at the time . . . be so available to helping and serving . . . et cetera."

Perhaps because we are exposed through the media to so much collective suffering—the ravaging of tribes and ethnicities, the horrible attacks on America on September 11, 2001, with the loss of so many, the random horrors of terrorism or natural disasters—we are also being refined as a species. Though some might say that too much exposure to suffering immures us to the pain of others, I disagree. Certainly the twentieth century and the opening of the twenty-first century have provided as large a canvas of observed suffering as any in history. But if we can remain conscious, refuse to turn our backs, and not shut down and ignore, the suffering of the world can open our hearts, deepen our compassion, and further dissolve the barriers that separate us from our companions on the journey. Purified of the illusion of isolation, we fearlessly soldier on, challenging defunct patterns of thinking and ancient social and political habits, and encouraging in ways large and small the social agenda of a mutually shared planet. In purging the sense of presumed "rightness" on the part of any nation or ideology, we open the way to a finer social fabric in which all cultures are seen as necessary and complementary.

Traditionally, mystics imbued with this sense of collective purpose purified the world by creating beauty in it. Saint Francis of Assisi rebuilt three ruined churches as part of his purification; Hildegard of Bingen planted gardens for God's enjoyment. Today, acts of public service, volunteerism, and philanthropy—random acts of kindness on a planetary scale—can fulfill our impulse for this kind of purification. Drives to clean up polluted rivers, restore crumbling monuments, rebuild inner-city neighborhoods, and reforest denuded mountain slopes are ways we can all engage in public purification. Perform these acts consciously, and we add to the grace of the universe.

Part of our process of release from old patterns and attitudes involves having someplace to go, some higher aspiration that serves as the lure for our becoming. Some are bred in the bone, for there is always the attracting force of our next level of development as we proceed through life stages from childhood onward. A child can always wistfully say, "When I grow up . . ." However, this plaintive cry really never ends. Whenever I ask an audience of people over thirty or forty or even sixty, "How many of you still don't know what you will be when you grow up?" virtually all of them raise their hands.

And so, as the spiritual mystic aims to achieve union with the One, the everyday mystic looks to have a more abundant and creative as well as useful life. Without the lure, the journey fails to satisfy; without the larger vision of the possible, one retreats into the questionable comforts of a life of serial monotony or worse. Champ's place in my life was one of grace and a kind of magic. He made sure that I did not stew too long in miserable cul-de-sacs and self-sabotaging emotions. In reflection, I realize he taught me that real release and transformation involve the "four Rs": route, rhythm, ritual, and rendezvous.

Champ was a superb route detector. He led me into greener pastures of friendship and discovery. Route refers to the path we choose to take—the routing through material-plane reality. Early in life we decide on a map—a point of view relative to what it's all about. The terrible and wonderful fact is that belief structures reality! Think of some of the belief routes that may have been inscribed on the cartography of your mind: "Life is hard and life is earnest . . . . You have to take the good with the bad, the ups with the downs. . . . Work hard, do things in the correct way, and maybe you'll get lucky—the break will happen, the lottery of life will be won. . . ."

Unfortunately, this route rarely leads to happiness. It belongs to a kind of attitude that comes from the long-held view that life is circumstantial—that we are given a set of circumstances and we have to find our way around or through them. The assumption here is that of ourselves we can do little, but through our dependencies on the authority of gods and institutions, we might gain a little letup. It denies us our ability to find creative solutions to the predicaments in our lives and to, more proactively, create the world of our dreams and visions.

The finer route assumes that life is an art form in which we learn to make beauty, create new patterns, find balance, and bring potentials into manifestation. One can live following the route of belief that the kingdom of heaven is not in some ephemeral afterlife but right within our midst, waiting to bud forth. We can even agree with Teilhard that we have the powers of world making, self making, life making. This is the route of routes, the path through the wonders of the kingdom. Here, the spiritual guide or the Champ in our lives is often the one who is given the role of finding richer, deeper routes into the many-tiered universe, so as to bring healing, wholing, and finer life for both individuals and the community. Of course, the pathway can have many forms: prayer, spiritual community, esoteric disciplines, the mystic path, or learning from the wise ones, including our elders, our children, and our animals. Above all, it is important to seek out and follow a route that carries one into new continents of spirit, where old moods are made redundant and new thought reigns.

Thus I would strongly suggest to you, the reader, that you rethink your routes. Which of them leads to the same old place of dull misery or psychic flatland? And which route would carry you into the kingdom of God, the realm of pure delight and radical possibility? As a practice, you may wish to draw the map of your old route and where it has led you. Then, in contrast, let yourself be inspired as you draw a new route informed by a sense of the possible. Make sure that it has many places to be of service, as well as being filled with spiritual practice. Then place yourself imaginatively in the new route and experience it until it becomes so real that the old, outmoded route becomes pale and diminished. Now you are back on track and have moved away from "spiritual drift." My good friend the minister Mary Manin Morrissey put it this way in one of her sermons I attended:

Spiritual drift doesn't happen overnight. It doesn't happen like a blow to the head. Spiritual drift results when we make small, continuous moves out of alignment with our true nature. We drift away from God in our thinking. Yet when we have thoughts and actions out of alignment with our nature, which is goodness, we don't feel right. There's unrest, and we begin to honor that inner nudge that prompts, pulls us, back to God. We can frame and form our lives so that every mistake can be turned into good.

Once agreed upon the route, one has to discover one's rhythm. Rhythm is music, beat, pulse, and pattern; most of all it is vibration. Everything we know is vibration, energy, frequency, and waves of electromagnetic charge moving out from us, between us, among us. You who are reading these words now are a vibration sender, a rhythm transmitter. These are charged up largely through your emotional circuits—the powerful transmitters located in the emotional centers of your body, brain, and being. Whenever you hear a drumbeat, you are aware of the waves going out and coming back.

45

On the macrocosmic scale, the world functions as an echo chamber to the drumbeat of your soul, of your feelings, and to the quality and tone of your transmission. What we put out in thought and emotional energy is what we get back in spades.

Champ was for me a melody of happiness. He vibrated sheer good will and the energy of joy. One could not be around him long before catching the music of his gladness. His tail was a baton of ebullience. This is the magic of rhythm—the knowledge and orchestration, the sheer arting, if you will, of what it is that we are transmitting, for then the beat will come back amplified. If ever we observe fine painters or composers creating their works of art, we see choice of color or notes, the astute use of their materials, the joyous and often inspired unfolding of their vision on canvas or music paper.

The same is true of conscious, artful transmission of our intentions. We are here in part to become artists in the field of manifesting our dreams, our intentions, and, yes, our inspirations. To do this, we can no more send out the gray fog of ambivalence or throw a mudball into the works than can the artist do the same to her or his canvas. Rather, we can make a conscious choice of working with symbolic materials, be they images, sounds, or smells—things that by their potent use cause us to practice artful intentionality and, therefore, manifestation. Like the native Americans and other indigenous people, we celebrate a desired possibility before it happens in real space and time. Rhythm is the mode that assures us what Helen Keller knew: that although the world is full of suffering, it is also full of the overcoming of it.

Which is why the third R, ritual, is so important to those who would have the finer life. Ritual comes from the Sanskrit word *rita*, meaning art, ritual, discipline, the dance, and the grace that allows us to move from one stage or plateau of life to the next. Rituals illumine our transitions and are the practices that create the field of possibility. They draw upon the powers of time, space, nature, and culture in such a way that we know we are the vehicle of the possibility, whether it be for making rain, healing, announcing a life transition like marriage, or declaring one's connectedness to high purpose or spiritual realities.

Champ, like many dogs, was a very good ritualist. He had a precise and well-rehearsed assemblage of actions and activities that clearly announced the next steps he wished us to take, be it for being fed, taken on a walk, or playtime. Then there were his ritual circlings, the lengthy turnings that preceded his settling down for sleep. He had specific chants and hoots to inform us of his desires, as well as strong looks and even more strongly beamed thoughts that left no doubt as to what we were to do next. I am certain that he created a powerful mental and emotional picture of what he required that went along with his wiggling, wagging, and woofing rites.

While I did not learn all I know about ritual from Champ, he did provide some very specific guidelines that translate well into human terms. To wit: Know where you want to go and give sensory evidence of it. This might mean honoring your path with flowers, music, and dance. Give the chosen path sacred space and time, so that you can move into a different state of being, drop your usual categories, and allow your consciousness to flow in magical space and time. You might wish to enact in a dramatic form the desired condition. Play it out both in the imagination as well as with gestures and movements that emulate what you desire to manifest. This is especially effective when stirring music plays as an accompaniment to your enactment. And above all, put yourself in touch with the grand and ancient tradition of making a new reality. Tell the story of this change in your life as if it already has happened, knowing that you are a channel for the budding forth of divine energy that always seeks new forms, innovative projects, inventive and passionate ways of being.

Route, rhythm, and ritual result in the fourth R, the rendezvous with the Divine Presence itself or in others. This meeting is the result of the heightened frequency in which one now exists as an amplified self able to enjoy a meeting with remarkable people as well as with Spirit. In my life, for example, not only was I having regular rendezvous with Dr. Biedermeir and Teilhard de Chardin, but also around the same time, I was having regular meetings with the great humanitarian Eleanor Roosevelt. As president of my high school student body, I and a number of other high school presidents were periodically getting together with this glorious woman to discuss educating young students to international awareness. She attended to each one of us as if we were very important to her and our remarks, however naive, held critical ideas. In her presence, we felt ourselves lifted to our better natures. On one of these occasions I even brought Champ along, and she was equally gracious to him.

There is a joke among my friends and acquaintances that goes, "If there is anyone in the world who you want to meet, just ask Jean—she probably knows them." This is an exaggeration, of course, but the fact is that my belief in the other three Rs has brought me to a place where I often meet and become friends with astonishing folk. This assumes the belief that we are all interconnected in spirit and that the right meeting, friendship, or service to give or be given is part of the deep artistry of this remarkable reality. The rendezvous with appropriate people and events is in essence the Divine placing itself before us in surprising ways. Finally, there is the openness to pure availability to the Source, the ultimate rendezvous: self to Self, spirit to Spirit, Godseed to GodSelf.

For me, Champ was expert in practicing the arts of releasing the habitual and opening to the unknown with joyous anticipation, and he helped me to do so. This is spiritual enchantment, and the task is to prepare one's mind, body, heart, and, above all, spirit so as to transcend the obstructions and negations of millennia and enter literally a new way of being that leads to a new form of reality. We are walking magnets, always attracting what it is we are sending out on the frequency vibrations. Thought patterns are magnets, and when amplified by emotional power they are powerful magnets. It is spiritual energy joined to emotional energy that has the power to bring about changes and manifestation in all manner of things—healing or abundance or social change or friendship or the success of any endeavor. This manner of attunement is the override of the collective negative vibrations that are coming to us all the time from a world in stress and fear and torment. Then perhaps we can one day attain the universal goodness and creativity that Teilhard dreamed and Champ portended.

I will never forget the time that I was so disheartened reading the newspapers in my room about the building of the hydrogen bomb. In despair I threw the paper across the room. Champ ran after it, nosed it about, and then, doing something he had never done since he was a pup, lifted his leg and let fly with a drenching comment.

"Thanks, Champ," I said, laughing. "That's telling it like it is."

CHAPTER THREE

Titan and Illumination

"**E**xcuse me, but that is the largest dog I've ever seen. What kind is it?"

"He's an Old English mastiff."

"Really? I've never heard of them. Is it a new breed?"

"Oh, no, it's one of the oldest continuing breeds around. They were first bred, we think, by the ancient Egyptians, who tried to get them to look like the lions. They've long been associated with royalty. The pharaoh Ramses wrote a hymn to his mastiff, and Charlemagne was said to have valued his mastiff above all his other animals. Julius Caesar brought them into Britain, and since the Brits were always crazy about dogs, they kept the breed going. The English Crusaders took them to the East and taught them how to sniff out and bite the Saracens. Mostly now, however, mastiffs take care of their masters and make excellent nannies."

"He must eat you out of house and home. What does he weigh?"

"Maybe 230, but his father weighed over 300 pounds. He's only two now but his head will continue to grow until he is five."

"Aren't you afraid to have such a fierce-looking dog in your house?"

"Fierce? Bend down and look in his eyes. Go ahead—he won't hurt you. Quite the contrary."

"Why, those are the kindest eyes I think I've ever seen. And, look, he's kissing me. He really likes me, doesn't he? It's strange. He makes me feel so good, like he's sending me blessings, kind of. It's like being around a saint or something."

That was a typical conversation when Titan and I were stopped by astonished viewers as we walked along the street. Giants among canines, mythic in appearance, mastiffs have long been idealized and anthropomorphized. Probably no other breed has been so celebrated in poetry and other literature as the mastiff—for its nobility, its fighting prowess, and as faithful friend, companion, and protector.

But bearing all that in mind, Titan was different—truly different—and in him was manifest the power of love in a degree that itself was mythic. It was not unusual for those who knew him to use such phrases as "an angel come down to Earth in a dog's body," and once, a famous Eastern holy man looked in his eyes and said, "He is a bodhisattva—a Buddha in training." Others found nothing incongruous in speaking of a "spirit" indwelling a dog's body for a time. And as for my husband and me, we felt singularly blessed to have such a presence in our life.

Titan seemed to have an inexhaustible reservoir of gladness, which he lavished on everyone he met. Once he even lost my husband, Bob, and I a research grant by lavishing too much love on a prospective grantor. We had already been scouted by the president of the foundation, and it looked like the grant was going to go through when, just for formality's sake, we were asked to entertain the vice president of the organization.

This formidable gentleman arrived and seemed to us the complete alien. His name was in the order of Worthington Windsor Raleigh, and there had never been a waspier WASP. A very large man, he wore a grey pinstripe suit, an old school tie, family crested cuff links, and a Phi Beta Kappa key dangling from his vest. From his beautifully coifed white hair to the high polish of his elegant shoes, he was not likely to be the optimal judge on our project to explore the nature of hypnotic trance and imagery.

We put out our best tea service and tried desperately to sound kosher, making up quasi-scientific terms to justify our research as we nervously served the tea. Worthington lifted his eyebrows in a well-bred sneer. Clearly, he was buying none of it. However, by dint of using up years of stored-up charm, Bob did manage to interest him in our work, and it was even looking like he would actually agree to sponsor our project when I decided to put the coup de grâce on the project by introducing my animal friends.

"Do you like dogs, Mr. Raleigh?"

"Oh, yes, very much. I've been breeding springer spaniels for over a decade now."

"Well then, let me bring out our wonderful mastiff . . ."

And with that Titan came into the room. He looked at Worthington. Worthington looked at him. A strange current moved between them. The two were clearly fascinated by each other. Had they known one another in a previous life? Titan's heavy three-foot-long tail began to swing in great arcs of joy, knocking the entire silver tea service off the table, cream now puddling on Worthington's pants, lemon curd cakes lending color to his gray suit. Then, for the first and last time in his career as a dog, Titan tried to place his Goliath body into somebody's lap. Unfortunately, that somebody was Worthington. Covering him with great soppy kisses, Titan also managed to rip the Phi Beta Kappa key from his vest. He couldn't stop loving this formidable gent.

Worthington went into some unknown emotion, caught between his attraction to Titan and his inability to stop the dog's immense demonstration of affection. It was the Titanic meeting the iceberg, only this time the iceberg lost. Our attempts to remove Titan from on top of the poor man only redoubled his ardor. Finally, in a herculean heave, Worthington managed to get up from under Titan and run out the door. I ran after him, and for some reason the only thing I could think to call out to his disheveled, departing form was, "But you haven't met my Airedale yet!"

Our grant was turned down.

Titan's enormous joie de vivre was particularly remarkable given the fact that he was in considerable pain for much of his life. Born with a spinal deformity, it appeared by the end of his first year that he would lose the use of his hind legs. Surgery was the only hope offered for what was repeatedly misdiagnosed as hip dysplasia. However, Bob and I cajoled and coerced that great genius of psychophysical functioning, Moshe Feldenkrais, to give us suggestions about how to remedy the defect. An Israeli who had no experience or liking of dogs, Moshe became fascinated with the case and determined a number of ways to retrain Titan in ways of walking.

With this information as well as other methods that Bob was able to devise, Bob worked with Titan twice a day for a year, teaching him different ways of moving and walking. For many years he was able to move enough to get around, though never without some degree of pain, until his condition worsened irredeemably toward the end of his life. Even then, when walking had become very difficult, Titan's joy and lovingness remained undiminished.

I used to hold a salon of ideas for about sixty people on Sundays, and he would drag himself over to each person, look lovingly in their eyes, and kiss them. Even if someone tried to trick him by hiding, Titan would always pull himself along on his front paws until he found them so that they, too, could be greeted and kissed. Then he would sit in the middle of the group, looking around the circle of people and giving *darshan*, or deep seeing. People would come from all over just to be "seen" by this dog, since he seemed to lift their cares and give them a sense of being unconditionally loved.

But there was something else that occurred in these meetings—something quite remarkable and of a nature that I have experienced neither before nor since. In the presence of Titan, our minds soared and many came up with ideas and projects that seemed far more developed than anything we had considered before. Inspiration ran rife through these meetings, brainstorms were common, the veils that obscured were lifted, and we felt as if we were being nourished in a field of knowledge and love that belonged to a larger reality. Could it be that Titan in his bodhisattva state of light and loving carried this larger reality that evoked cosmic means, higher intelligence?

People who attended these meetings began to call me up to ask whether they could have private sittings with my dog since his presence seemed to bring forth their finest thought. I will never forget the sight of an eminent bald philosopher sitting on the rug, holding hands with Titan while a tape recorder preserved the concepts inspired by this illumined canine. When I interrupted this communion for a moment to bring the philosopher a cup of tea, I asked him why he got so intellectually stimulated in the presence of Titan. He replied in some wonderment, "It's as if there are two realities here: the existential one of this marvelous dog in front of me and an essential one that is on a continuum with the source mind of the universe." Titan just thumped his huge tail and glowed.

Titan was a natural rescuer, seeking out people who were in emotional distress and looking at them until they felt a great wave of peace come upon them. But he also went out and physically rescued people on a number of occasions. There was the time when he and I were walking in a forest, and I fell down the hill and badly sprained my ankle. Even though this was at a point in his life when Titan was walking only with the greatest of pain, he somehow managed to climb down the hill, nose me up with his huge head, and drag me up the hill. All the way home he kept his body close to mine for support, and I leaned on him in order to walk. Needless to say, from this exertion he was not himself able to walk for the next several weeks.

Then there was the incident with Bob's mother, Kay Masters. She had had a laryngectomy and was only able to speak in a very strange and harsh tone using a voice machine. Oliver, my beloved Airedale, who had the most sensitive hearing, finally couldn't stand the sound of her voice any more and sprang for her as she was seated in a wheelchair. In that same instant, Titan's huge golden body hurtled through the air, almost as if he had taken flight, and smashed Oliver to the floor, holding him down with his great paw until we could wheel Kay away. After that, as long as she visited with us, Titan stayed constantly at my mother-in-law's side, sleeping at night at the foot of her bed. The Airedale had leaped without any forewarning, we noticed, but Titan must have moved in exactly the same instant, or even just before, having picked up Oliver's intention telepathically.

This incident caused lasting trouble, since afterward Titan was determined to fight and perhaps kill Oliver, something he several times almost accomplished. They could never again be together for a moment, a fact that made life difficult for all as we always had to be on top of which dog was on what side of a door at every moment. One of the shadow sides of the mastiff is that in spite of their loving nature, once they have decided on someone's (animal or human) moral character, they never forget it and seek to root out what they see as evil, should any occasion arise. (Of course, this can also be a characteristic of certain mystics—witness the crusty and irascible demeanor of certain enlightened monks.)

Titan's behavior as regards Oliver was curious given that in general his reverence for life was positively worthy of missionary physician Albert Schweitzer. If either Bob or I so much as swatted a fly, we would get a disapproving look from him, whereupon he would get up and leave the room. In experimenting to verify our observations of this behavior, we also observed on many occasions that he would get up and leave with a reproachful look if we even *thought about* such an action. And should he be out in the dog yard, Titan would get up and move to a far corner of the yard, facing away from us, when we decided to swat a fly. We demonstrated this often to others, and it seemed clear in this instance as in others that he received some images as they formed in our minds, as well as by other "extrasensory" means.

Titan had many admirers, one of whom was the anthropologist Margaret Mead, who often came and stayed with us. A person of acute senses who noticed everything, she said, "He has the most fragrant and pleasant breath that I've ever experienced." To which my husband replied, "The odor of sanctity is no mere metaphor, Margaret."

Margaret used to like to creep up on Titan when he was asleep. She enjoyed, she said, his sonorous snores, which resembled the "songs" of the humpback whales. But mostly, Margaret, along with many others, liked to just sit in his company and be present to his deep seeing. "It rests me," she said, "being around this big dog. I am such a public person, and have so much stuff projected onto me, that it rests me to be seen so completely for who and what I truly am."

Titan was a phenomenon of loving, a being of such grace and kindness, and of the warmest sympathy, that he was said to glow. His nature and presence gave a sense of what is known in the mystical life as the stage of "illumination." In this state, mind and body are transduced for a while into another domain of being. In the classical experience, one is literally flooded with light, crowned by halos, suffused in golden mosaics, entranced by the play of light in nature. It is as if, as a result of the inward changes, the mystic's sensible experience is also illumined. The light brings with it a sense of infinite love. In fact, the very nature of the light is said to be love.

During the time in this state, one sees beauty and meaning, pattern and loving connection everywhere, and yet when ordinary consciousness returns, one is able to go about daily work. Even then, the perspective of luminosity infuses everyday activities with joy and an appreciation of the splendor of existence. Most importantly, one falls into loving all whom one meets, as Titan did, and one inspires in them a loving response and a sense of well-being.

In the human realm, one feels oneself to be sharing in the knowledge, experience, and loving of the universe—the mind and heart of being itself. With advanced states of illumination, it seems that everything is clearly known and seen to be connected to everything else. All beings, realities, arts, sciences, and relationships,

Nature herself, and even the vast workings of the cosmos can selectively be downloaded to one's local mind. Creativity blooms, and one seems to have the ready answer, the right word or formula of grace. Illumination is not limited to the mystic and is often synonymous with the enhanced creativity sought by artists, writers, visionaries, scientists, and other creative folk. But what mystics tend to do that nonmystical creative people do not is to sustain and live in the light so that they are filled with such love and joy that their state becomes an inspiration to others, as was the case with the saintly Titan.

Many have wondered just where all this light is coming from. I, for one, suspect this state to be natural and innate because, quite simply, we are made out of light. We are in part photonic beings: our very substance is made up of fermions—that is, particles of electrons and fields of matter—and bosons—that is, photons and fields of force or energy that emerge out of a universe that holds all potentiality.

In fact, it would seem that our physical world, including our bodies, is unfolding at the speed of light out of realms beyond space-time as a manifestation of light. Physics has long recognized that under the right circumstances, light and matter can switch identities. Matter can be considered as condensed or frozen light. By light we mean the entire electromagnetic spectrum, not just the octave that we experience as visible light.

And what is light? It is that quality or tool by which we have gained almost all the knowledge we have about the universe. There are new speculations that light itself belongs to an order that underlies but is beyond the space-and-time universe. What we consider light may be consonant with the mind of the universe, the Godmind that holds the patterns that guide our growth, our unfolding, even our creativity. Therefore, those who experience this transcendent light are said to be illumined or "en-lightened" because they are living from the perspective of God. This holds huge consequences for the nature of our consciousness. Matter and light then serve to orchestrate the foreground and the background of awareness.

We might understand the illumination that comes of high creativity or mystical insight as moving from the foreground of everyday reality to the background of consciousness, wherein the light of all being abides. This would account for the mystic's experience of an unfathomable oceanic depth beyond depth and of her or his ability to gather in perceptions from "elsewhere." This information appears to transcend local time and space, culture and personality.

This awareness extends not only to our physical systems, but dives deep into the larger dynamic system of which our physical reality is a part. Putting it in terms of quantum physics, it is a knowledge of not only the particle but also the wave. Thus the deepest values, purposes, and patterns for life, the richest potential coding for existence, and the source level of creative patterns and innovative actions and ideas are fathomed when we are in that state. For it is then that we apprehend with such a simultaneity of knowings that we can be said to have grasped the whole of anything or anybody. In this state of direct knowledge, there is a certainty, a clarity and precision, a rightness that transcends all ordinary awareness.

Too often in Western culture, we diagnose and pathologize our creative or spiritual geniuses instead of recognizing that they have simply moved from the foreground to the background, from local to nonlocal consciousness for a while. When I've lived and studied with indigenous people—Maoris, Australian Aborigines,

Native Americans, African tribal societies—I find that generally they, like our animal companions, do not make a great distinction between interior and exterior reality; Great Nature without is reflected in even greater nature within. Thus these peoples tend to have a sense of a deep ecology between their inward and outward worlds. As a result, they are often far more cherishing and nourishing than we are of those who adventure for a time into inward worlds. They know the value of these worlds and take care of the traveler until she or he returns. Because the inward journey has been honored and given status, the journeyer often returns bearing gifts—new songs or stories, dances, suggestions for planting, a gift of healing, even a radical initiative.

What is true of the illumination of individuals is also true of cultures and, by extension, of the planet. Unprecedented trauma and unequaled challenge have created the conditions for an opening in the foreground of everyday existence and a rising of the background of consciousness and psyche, of high pattern and deep purpose. Something is rising out of the light of divine no-thingness that contains the seeds and codings of the next step of our planetary unfolding.

Consider the effect of the world's woundings, each of which is affecting the psyche of nations as well as our own souls, demanding of us action of mythic and even mystic proportions. Presently, a trauma of worldwide dimensions is threatening all lifeforms as well as the very stability of our planet's features. Through mammoth levels of pollution brought about by industrial, agricultural, and pharmaceutical poisons, the wasteland increases, deformities grow, the food chain is compromised, the water tables sink. With this onslaught comes whole-scale species extinction, ultraviolet bombardment, global warming, polar meltdown, and drastic changes in the wind systems and ocean currents. Temperatures soar and plunge apocalyptically, the deserts gallop through fading green belts, the ecology collapses. It's a daunting prospect.

However, it may well be that all of us alive today self-selected to be born in this time of stupendous ecological challenge so as to be part of the process of remaking consciousness and thus of rescuing the world. Nothing less than illumination and love expressed on a global scale will allow us to catch the vision wave of a better future and make the hard changes it demands.

A few years ago, an Australian friend of mine sat brooding one morning under a giant tree that was faced with extinction. Cutters from a huge transnational lumber company were coming later that day to take out the tree and others in that part of an old-growth forest in the region in which she lived. Suddenly my friend felt herself to be in all the trees, illumined by Nature herself. She knew herself as tree and ground, sky and earth. She felt her blood flow in the veins of the leaves, knew herself to be hundreds of years old like the tree she was nestling against. This went on for what seemed like aeons, although when she looked at her watch, she discovered that only a few minutes had passed.

She knew instantly what she would have to do. She began to climb the tree, up fifty feet and more. She would live in the tree and refuse to come down until the company agreed to cease cutting that part of the forest. Her friends sent up living supplies and a small platform to make her comfortable. The cutters came, threatened, and went away. Soon people from all over the island showed up to protect her, becoming part of the movement to save this ancient forest. Each day the cutters returned, and each day they faced more and more people sitting in front of their giant machines, refusing to move. My friend lived in the tree for many weeks, and a forest was saved at that time. One instant of illumination had galvanized a movement throughout the region to protect the forests and preserve a piece of the natural world.

The illumined ones can take any form—a man, a woman, a child, an elder, or even a dog. The quality that most distinguishes them, as Titan so profoundly exemplified, is not just their radiance but their loving nature. In their presence there is no estrangement, nothing to fear, and everything to accept. They serve as midwives of souls, beloved healers who regard us with such affection and esteem that what is best and deepest in us is called forth. This is the divine assignment of those illumined ones: to live in and express love and thereby to inspire higher purpose, deeper consciousness.

Titan was a guide to goodness. In his presence people saw themselves and their role on Earth in a new way. I like to believe that he was indeed what the visiting Eastern holy man called a bodhisattva. And it is the bodhisattva ideal to help others discover their spiritual nature and the unique gifts they have to offer. Certainly, this was the effect that Titan had on so many. He served as a light on the path to the discovering of their higher natures.

The way of the bodhisattva is one of living out of one's essential God-given, or Buddha, nature. It is the path of recognizing one's spiritual genes and opening up to one's unique tasks in a spiritually conscious universe. It is the path of applied illumination. The word *bodhisattva* comes from the Sanskrit roots *bodhi,* meaning awakening or enlightenment, and *sattva,* meaning sentient being. *Sattva* has also been translated as the creative and resolute intention to wake up. In the traditional Buddhist belief, bodhisattvas are those whose entire life, and even lives, are dedicated to helping all and everything to wake up to the glory of their beingness. Having known the sheer splendor of the oneness of life and spirit, they feel the need to spread the word, offer help to those who are suffering, guide others to a path of new possibilities, and be companions and friends on the road of life. Bodhisattvas differ from Buddhas in that they don't enter nirvana until they have helped all beings everywhere to attain liberation.

In Mahayana Buddhism, one of the two major Buddhist traditions, the bodhisattva is the heroic ideal, the evolutionary promise inherent in all human beings. Lest that seem like the tallest of all tall orders, remember that bodhisattvas also believe in the ultimate unity of all being and the fact that not one of us is really apart from the other. Thus in helping all beings, they evince the most total and complete compassion for themselves.

Bodhisattvas have been described as "enlightening, radiant beings who exist in innumerable forms, valiantly functioning in helpful ways right in the midst of the busy-ness of the world."[1] They can be awesome in their radiant presence, their creativity, and their illuminating wisdom. But they can also be as ordinary as the checker at the supermarket, your third-grade teacher, the bus driver, and, yes, even your lawyer. And don't forget your pet. When I once asked a large group how many thought that they had known people who were bodhisattvas, only a few hands went up. Then when I asked if a pet they had known had been a bodhisattva, a great many hands went up.

Thus they can be found in every tradition, age, place, and even species. When it comes to humans, however, to be a bodhisattva does not mean that our life has been saintly; we may have even been a hell-raiser and a royal pill at some point in our life. In fact, many bodhisattva types have had flawed and shadowed careers at one time or another—witness Titan's dedication to cleansing the world of the Airedale. Bodhisattvas have known the suffering and delusions of the world and fallen prey to them, just as we all have. What is different is that out of their experience has grown a deep concern and compassion for their fellow travelers on life's path. They do not hide out, roiling in regret and self-blame. Instead, they harvest their shadows so as to bring forth a greater good; think of it as the manure you put on the soil of your nature to grow a finer crop of goodness.

Bodhisattvas help us see ourselves, including how we may be a blessing to society. They show us that working on ourselves and in the world are not separate enterprises. Like Titan in the canine world, a wonderful illustration of a human bodhisattva is my friend Laura, whose daily life exemplifies this process.

When Laura awakens in the morning, she reflects on her dreams, teasing out their messages or teachings. Her shower is a conscious cleansing and refreshing of all her senses. Standing under the spray of water, she sets her intention for the day: "Great Spirit, let me be a blessing to someone today." For her morning meditation she walks through her garden, wonderfully aware of breeze and birds, the greening power of the earth, the cast of the sky, her neighbor's face as she greets him. She remembers a juicy bit of gossip that she heard about another neighbor, opens her mouth to relate it, but then says an inner "No!" to the impulse, aware of the long-term consequences of loose speech.

After savoring each bite of her buttery omelette, the cool citrus tang of her orange juice, and the heady intensity of freshly brewed coffee, she looks at the paper. She turns first to the good news of arts and theater in her community, of people helping people, even the funny papers. Only then with a positive mind does she read about wars and mayhem. These she considers with a balanced eye, looking always for the larger story of what is trying to happen in the world. She writes a check to help refugees in a war-torn country.

Ecologically conscious, she takes the bus to work and always smiles at fellow passengers, giving them a subtle boost for the day. The same smile greets the office staff. Laura is a financial analyst, and people come to her to talk about money. She views the financial culture as an opportunity for awakening and her clients as seekers who require gentle guidance as to what they really need. When one comes to see her that afternoon, she listens to what he is saying as well as to what he is not. Because of her genuine human engagement, her clients open up and tell her about their deeper hopes and dreams. She understands that money is basically energy, a way to make things happen, and she brings this understanding to each decision she makes.

After work Laura goes to her aikido class. On the mat, she works to meld her energy with that of her partner so that the techniques they practice become a complex dance of subtly shifting awareness. Then she eats dinner with a group of single mothers she is mentoring. She regards them not only as women in difficulty but as peers, from whom she can learn much. Conversation flows easily, as she shares with them difficult times in her life—a divorce, a betrayal, how healing has happened.

When her day is done, she greets her home like the old friend it is. She waters the plants, seeing them as fellow beings who happen not to be mobile or particularly talkative. She calls her fiancé, who lives in another city. They share their days and a good deal of love talk. In a blissful state, she prepares for bed, reflecting on the fullness of her life; it becomes for her a revelation of the divinity that animates all things. With a prayer for the good of everyone and thankfulness for the blessings of the day, she drifts off to sleep, perhaps to meet in her dreams her divine inner companion.

Laura never met Titan, but her life unfolds as if she had. Her inspiration comes from moving beyond betrayal and hardship and dedicating her life to living each day as spiritual exercise and seeing all people as gods-in-hiding. She profoundly does her human home-work and regards each moment as an opportunity for enlight-enment. She is love in action and in this is as close to Titan's hugely loving presence as any human I have ever known.

While both of these beings are on the extreme end of the bodhisattva scale, it is certainly possible to follow their example to some degree. All of us have an innate yearning for natural good-ness, kindness, active compassion. All have the instinct for loving, which is perhaps the most important of all. Indeed, above every-thing else, the main lesson the bodhisattva Titan taught me is that the supreme activity is to love and then to love some more. For love changes everything—the way we see, think, dream, act, en-gage the world, serve others, and even transcend our local selves. Love is the source of most songs, poetry, writing, dreaming, hu-man folly, and human glory. It is what wakes us up, keeps us going. As we love more, we see and accept more, honoring each other's pain, struggle, and path. Like Titan, we give and receive *darshan*—the loving look that empowers while it deepens. With love we become illumined and thus more intelligent and creative, for we are open to the patterns of intelligence from the whole network of life. We come to glimpse the wonder of life in its infinite forms and the wonder that is within us.

Quite simply, with love we exceed our local conditions—we evolve. Without love we probably would not have gotten beyond the primordial globules floating in an early ocean. No, even earlier: without love we would not have flung ourselves forward in the big bang, seeking partners and lovers in creation.

Those in the illumined state often tell us that the universe in all its parts is alive and that love is its life force. There are waves of thought, energy, and emotion coming from everything in the universe toward us, and we are radiant with the same. Thus reality is a vast interplay in which everything is affected by everything else in the most literal sense. After all, the universe grows by its connections and its attractions—atoms to atoms, molecules to molecules, bodies to bodies, groups to groups, nations to nations, and finally our planet to the other heavenly bodies that make up our cosmos, and they to each other. These affections and connections are part of the Godbeing finding the forms of its relationships through the love that moves the sun and all the stars. And that is why those who enter into the primordial primacy of relationship to God or Spirit as the Beloved find that this then spills over to all things, like Francis of Assisi loving and rescuing a worm on the road or accepting into his fold a former criminal no one else wanted.

The most natural ways of loving are all around us. For example, we love our gardens, giving them attention and devotion, and they love us back by producing fruit, flowers, and fascinating weeds. The same is true of our dogs, cats, horses, birds, and other domesticated creatures. If you or I had received the same quality of loving regard and empowerment that we give to our animals, there is no telling how evolved our lives would be. Likewise, if we gave to each other the quality of attention and devotion that we give to our gardens, people would bloom—and they would bloom in the garden of our lives as we would bloom in theirs. With our animals and our gardens we are wise enough to know that we must give attention, devotion, and awareness in order to get a loving response, but with human relationships for some reason we expect far less of ourselves.

The issue, then, is one of conscious loving. Unfortunately, we are brought up to think that love is something that happens to us—that it is a startle, an astonishment, a bolt from the blue, an unexpected grace. That is undoubtedly true in part, but it puts us in a passive relationship to what is actually a dynamo of vibrant giving and receiving. To participate in that dynamo we have to make conscious choices to plug in, to be conduits of this marvelous power. And that means to make conscious choices for active loving.

Titan (with one exception) saw every contact as occasion for giving affection. Even when he was asleep, if someone passed near his long golden body his great tail would thump a "Glad you are here" greeting. Should he wake up, he would heave up his pain-ridden body to greet you, pulling himself along on his front feet in order to give you a kiss. With Titan, love exceeded pain, tenderness overcame agony. Now that's an illumined being.

How do we generate such energy of loving in ourselves and our own lives? Practice, practice, practice. The Hindus and Buddhists have four beautiful goals for a loving life. They include qualities I will translate as

1. loving-kindness;

2. heart compassion;

3. the willingness to allow oneself to be or become happy because someone else is happy (no matter what levels of unhappiness one has been feeling);

4. the hardest one for most of us: allowing oneself to maintain and be in a state of loving, easy equanimity when others are behaving like wretches.

The general method of practice recommended for reaching these estimable goals involves ever deepening forms of meditation. I would add a process drawn from my observation of Titan: Catch the movement of love wherever you find it. Cultivate that sweet energy and allow it to emanate in occasions both simple and profound. Above all, know the world as lover, world as self.

Finally, what about achieving a state of creative or mystical illumination? How can we become more like my dog? How do we go about it? Obviously, it differs from person to person. But there are practices that prepare the mind for receiving this gift. They involve the willing shift of perspective from local seeing to God's-eye seeing expressed in the words of a treatise of German mystic Meister Eckhart: "The eye by which I see God is the same eye by which God sees me."

To make this shift from human eye to spiritual eye involves imagining that transcendent eye deep within you. As you follow your breathing, the light from that eye expands with each breath, becoming more intense and brighter as it gradually fills all parts of you. Eventually you seem to be this eye, a luminous oval. You are a being of light. You are embedded light.

Now view planet Earth with your eyes of limitless light. You can look at our current ecological crisis and see through it, see its connection to every other situation. You can look at every person who has been in your life and see or know, with a heart of great compassion, the things that have caused them to suffer, the things that have caused them to grow. You know their pains and their joys, for in this beingness of light nothing is hidden. You see the continuous changing of things and yet the essential reality and unity of all being. Situations in your life are illumined now from the place of light, and it may be that you begin to see them with greater understanding and find unique solutions from this place of creative illumination. You look into world's pain and need, and do the same.

You are looking at these things from the vantage of the fathomless depths of that Oneness that is the transcendent light. And the light that is embedded in you burns deeper and brighter because you are in that field of light. From this moment, if you choose, you will always have access to your beingness of light, for you know now that, as Titan so graciously demonstrated, the state of illumination is a natural form within you.

CHAPTER FOUR

Voices and Visions
with the Airedale Tribe

My best friend was moving to the West Coast of the United States and decided to replace herself in my daily life with a dog. Moreover, she decided to replace herself with a breed that looked like her. But where would we find a sturdy, rather long-nosed, brownish-reddish curly haired, bright-eyed version of her? After investigating many breeds, she found that the one who most resembled her was the Airedale. So off we went to the kennel, and there we discovered little Oliver, who became my next best friend.

Soon I was to discover that the resemblance between Oliver and my human friend continued in many other ways. Both could be remarkably shaggy for months on end and then suddenly appear gorgeously well groomed. Both were intellectual, talkative, and always seeking out new skills and new projects. Both were exceedingly versatile and given to reconciling seeming polarities—the human, being a Jewish Buddhist as well as a scientist-mystic, while the dog could sing opera as well as catch and throw Frisbees. Each had a genius for friendship and a penchant for soulful communion.

When he was about four months old, Oliver took to placing

his paws on my knees, boosting himself to eye level, and staring at me with a terrible intensity and without blinking. Then he would begin to croon softly, and the message would come through: "I am much more than you think I am. And if you will give me the care and attention I need, I will prove this to you."

It was about this time that my friend, then living in Berkeley, was studying Tibetan Buddhist practices with the aim of transcending the limits of her human condition. Both dog and human seemed all their lives (as of this writing my human friend still lives and thrives) to be in search of the next stage of their respective evolutions, to be perpetually "transitional" beings—not quite dog or human but not yet something else. My human friend wondered about karma and previous life connections; my Airedale dreamed of it, or so it seemed to me.

One afternoon I had just lain down to take a nap when Oliver jumped up on the bed and curled his body next to mine. We were both sweetly snoozing when suddenly I found myself in a dream— Oliver's dream—in which I had no part but was an observer. It began as what one would think of as a typical dog dream: green grass passing rapidly beneath one's running body. But then it changed, and the dream became the story of a young man in a boater straw hat who had fallen deeply in love with a petite blonde girl. In the course of the dream the girl jilted him, and so great was his sorrow that he committed suicide.

Oliver awoke from our "shared" dream very disturbed and fell into a funk for the rest of the day. He would neither eat nor drink, but only stare at the wall and occasionally let loose with long melancholy sighs. He seemed to have had a vision in his dream that deeply disturbed him, and I, for one, was perplexed as to what this might mean.

Whereas my friend was inclined toward men younger than herself, Oliver would develop fixations on certain very young women that were poignant in the depth and fervor of feeling both given and received. The most intense of his relationships involved Janice, a petite blonde girl of eighteen who came to be our summer housekeeper when he was a year and a half. The moment she came through the door for the first time, Oliver leapt to attention, rapture in his eyes, then proceeded to try to talk and tell her something. He followed her faithfully throughout the months she spent with us, refusing to let her out of his sight. Rarely have I ever seen anyone so passionately in love as Oliver that golden summer.

Janice herself, much bemused by her love-besotted swain, returned a portion of his vast affection. "It is just like having a special boyfriend," she said. One day she asked him in my presence, "Oliver, do you want to marry me?" Oliver, in answer, placed his paws on her shoulders and kissed her tenderly on the lips. When Janice returned to college in Kansas in September, Oliver went into several months of mourning—sitting near her chair in grief, howling, and pulling out as much of his hair as he could reach with his teeth.

The following summer Janice returned, and the whole emotional drama was played out again, with Oliver even more in love if that was possible. This year, however, Janice had gotten herself engaged, and when her fiancé came for a visit and Oliver found him with his arms around her, it was only with the greatest of physical efforts that we dissuaded the Airedale not to kill his rival. Janice worked for us only those two summers, sending her dramatic sister Peggy in her place as our housekeeper. When she married her fiancé, she asked only for a large picture of Oliver and placed it prominently in her new home.

Unlike my human best friend, Oliver was a warrior at heart, and for the first few years of his life he lived in an uneasy truce around the mastiff Titan. Oliver and Titan would be resting quietly when suddenly Oliver would slowly raise his head and remember that he couldn't abide Titan. He would send out war signals on the ESP band, which would be immediately picked up by Titan. Tails would stiffen, and if they were outside, our fourteen cats would hone in on the signal and divide themselves between each dog, rubbing against their legs and lifting their lithe bodies to touch the combatants' faces in a vain effort at peacekeeping.

Like the ethnic groups of certain nations, there was nothing but bred-in-the-bone enmity between mastiff and Airedale, and the canine version of the battle of Agincourt would erupt. Hoses, pots of ice water, shouting—nothing could stop them. Once, Bob had to uproot a small tree to whack down on their heads to get them to quit. Another time he foolishly got caught in the middle as Oliver was sailing toward Titan and caught the full crunch of the Airedale's teeth on his arm. To this day he wears a necklace of bite scars on his flesh.

Finally, their battles royal got so gigantic, and the vet bills from these engagements so high, that we had to set up a series of closed doors between the two dogs. Bob and I were always calling each other on the phone from different ends of house to find out where each animal was located at any given moment. Only our third dog at the time, the white boxer Moondog, could be trusted with either of them. On more than several occasions our efforts failed—the wrong door was opened, and the house was soon a shambles of fur, blood, and broken furniture. It was a wonder that Oliver held his own and never gave up, seeing that the mastiff outweighed him by about 160 pounds. But, then, Airedales are famous for that.

Interesting enough, Oliver was always shocked and ashamed of himself after these episodes, shaking his head as if to say, "Did I really have to do that?" This shame would also occur after a spontaneous bout of trying to hump Moondog. Oliver actually seemed appalled at his own doggie nature. It was then that his efforts to be a transitional dog would become more purposeful.

For years, Oliver and I had been famous for our duets. He would accompany me in his stunning tenor as I sang Italian opera. This was no dog howling in agony over high notes; this was a dog who truly loved to sing, who initiated the songfest and urged me to join him on various occasions. One day when he was around ten years old, Oliver came up to me wagging his tail madly, vocalizing in an operatic manner, and looking at me meaningfully.

I sensed that he was trying to impart some critical message. "Oliver, what is it you want?" I asked. "Do you want to sing? We always sing. What are you trying to tell me?"

Oliver stopped wagging his tail and looked thoughtful, clearly trying to figure out how to communicate what he had in mind. At last he began to sing, but with a brilliant clarity, holding a perfect note without wavering. At that moment my mind meshed with his, and I knew what he wanted. "You want to sing on key, don't you?" His tail signaled the affirmative.

I launched into an aria from *Rigoletto*. Oliver waited for his chance, and when I hit a high C, he attempted an exact emulation. "AHHOOOOOO," he sang with much feeling and technical brilliance. We continued singing together for a while—a mysterious interface between human and dog, carried by the music of Verdi into interspecies consonance. When we ended, I was so excited that I ran to get my husband. When I launched again into the aria with Bob looking on, Oliver backed away grumbling, clearly unwilling to share our secret.

The following day, Oliver came up to me again, his tail flagging yet another brave notion. "What do you want to do today, Oliver? Send me the thought." Oliver opened his mouth and cut loose with a weird barrage of growls, hoots, and whines that seemed an attempt at speech.

"You want to speak, is that it?" Oliver's tail signified the affirmative. "OK. Try my name: JEAN. JEEEEAAN." In response, Oliver worked his jaws laboriously but produced only a disappointing squeak. Suddenly, he lay on his back as if he knew that only in that position could he make truer sounds.

"JEEEEAN," I encouraged him.

"EEEEEEE," Oliver responded.

"That's just great. Now try your name: O-LI-VER."

"RAAAAH GRRRRRR," Oliver replied. "RAAAAAH GRRRRRR!"

I was wild with excitement—a new boundary had been crossed! Oliver and I had transcended the great linguistic divide between human and beast. By this point in my professional life, I had held sign-language conversations with Washoe the chimpanzee, who was highly trained to communicate with hand signals, and had spent time swimming with and being taught elaborate games by dolphins, but never before had I reached such an unexpected and emotionally charged breakthrough.

Again I ran to get my husband. But alas, as before, all that Oliver would do with Bob present was cast baleful glances at me and move away, complaining and muttering in dogspeak, "Raaaoow, raaaaow, raaaow, raaaaow, raaaow . . ."

One might think it a far stretch that Oliver could really have been trying to say my name and his. Was this just my ear interpreting his earnest attempts in favor of English sounds? Maybe, but then again, maybe not. We humans often garble our yearnings in inchoate speech, sputter our expressions of love and rage, and strive to touch transcendence in our own working jaws. When I reflect on what my prayers must sound like to God, it also probably appears like something in the order of "RAAAAH GRRRRRR."

Oliver also demonstrated his wish to surpass himself in his efforts at construction. A friend, Norman, offered to build me a cottage on our property where I could find the quiet and space to do my writing. For some reason Norman and Oliver got along famously, possibly because Norman treated Oliver as an intelligent person, shared with him his ideas on life, and invited him to join him as he built the little cottage. Norman would lay out the materials—the boards and the stones that would go into the foundation—carefully telling Oliver the name for each. Then, when he needed a board he would say, "Oliver, bring me a two-by-four," and Oliver would quickly go and pull a board over to Norman. If Norman asked for a stone, Oliver would carefully choose one and, if it was too heavy to carry, do what he could to push it in the direction of his friend.

"Thank you, Oliver," Norman would praise as he helped Oliver push the stone the last few feet. "You are a mighty fine worker." You could almost see Oliver's chest swell with pride.

Together the two builders worked on that house for some six months. Oliver left his doghouse and was at the door at 6 A.M. every morning, eager to go to work. Norman would share his lunch with him, and neither dog nor man would quit until after dark. When the house was finished, Oliver fell into a depression, for it seemed that there was no further way to prove himself. It was then that I decided to take him on a vision quest.

I had come to realize that dogs, as our constant companions, had become "liminal." We humans are by nature liminal beings, meaning we are often betwixt and between one reality and another. Apart from occasional raptures, going mildly mad, or falling in love, we regularly experience this state in the moments just before falling asleep or just after waking up. It is then particularly that voices and visions of the hynagogic state can appear before our liminal minds to amuse or inspire us. By learning to work with this imagery, we can employ it for the sake of greater vision and problem solving. It is a gift of the unconscious, and we can often regain its insights through meditation and the altering of our minds in ways that allow us to travel beneath the surface crust of consciousness.

One of the most effective ways of discovering the truth of one's condition is the formal vision quest. Long known as a way to deepen and explore the meaning of one's life journey, it has assumed new importance and growing acceptance in our time. Vision quests are especially effective for adolescents as rites of passage, during which young people release their childhood and its associations, and are reborn to adulthood and its responsibilities and privileges. Prepared by guides, questers of any age drum and fast and pray, walk through difficult terrain, and then sit and wait and listen.

For a long time, nothing out of the ordinary may happen. Doubts arise as to the purpose of the whole enterprise, but one persists and deepens one's prayers. After a while, the passing forms of nature assume meaning and direction. A hawk flies over, and it is a prophetic annunciation. In the midst of dryness and thirst rains fall, and one knows that nourishment is nigh. Then in the middle of the night, a bear appears. Is it real or not? One never knows, but it has power and presence. Strength is imparted, along with a glimmer of a path. Closing one's eyes, one observes that the path remains. One follows it into inward worlds, the bear beckoning one forward. One passes scenes from one's life and enters a domain outside of time. Choices are shown, gifts are given. One returns enhanced and filled with the sense of having moved from novice to initiate.

Would that the world could engage in such visioning on a planetwide scale! Everyone tuned to presence and to the mystery that is there; the Spirit, like gathering wind, moving through all hearts; a vision of what may be, touching all minds.

And so I embarked with Oliver on such a quest, as much for his sake as for mine. I figured that Great Nature would treat us equally since we were equally in need of some revelation. Together we climbed a nearby mountain and sat down, me meditating, he musing on the distant landscape. I abstained from food, allowing myself only a little water, but did not require him to do so. Oliver stayed strangely quiet for a dog that was used to barking at nothing. Even when the large hawks that inhabited this mountain flew over, he regarded them mildly and uncharacteristically made no move to jump after them. The rains came and he snuggled closer; the rains went and we continued waiting.

For two days we maintained our vigil. Then a song began coming from all around where we were sitting—a strange, sweet melody, wordless and yet imparting wisdom. It seemed to say that there is One Life and that this Life is God, and that this Life circulates around the mountain, down in the valley, in the sky above and the ground beneath, in me, and in Oliver as well. And that this Life is love, which changes weakness into strength, fear into faith. There was more. Ideas came streaming in on that song, ideas that would figure in many later activities and books. I turned on a tape recorder I had brought along should I have any inspiration that needed recording—surely the sound would be captured on tape, I thought.

The song grew stronger and clearly Oliver heard it too, for suddenly he lifted his head and began to sing along. It was not his usual singing such as we did in our operatic duos. It was a kind of keening ecstasy—his soul set to music, Nature telling her truth through his nature. A little later we walked down the mountain, I feeling I had received much more than I had expected, Oliver curiously content, in fact with a peacefulness about him that I had never seen before. In the months remaining to his life he was unusually happy—he had been to the mountain.

People ask me what was on the tape recorder during the time of the song. I have to answer, "Nothing, but then again, everything. For Oliver's song sang it all."

About two months after our quest, Oliver died. I was away teaching in California the night he passed on, but I got an earful as soon as I returned home. My housekeeper at that time, Elizabeth Oloo, was a Kenyan woman studying for her masters degree in child development at the local university. She reported to me that right after Oliver died, she woke up to find him in her room, no longer in dog shape but rather as "a young man without his skin on who smiled and waved at [her] and then disappeared."

Had Oliver finally mastered the game of transition? Or was this just Elizabeth's native belief system projecting a vision of animals becoming human, that occurs in any number of African folktales? Whatever it was, I fell into mourning, and Bob would find me late at night sitting in my office staring at a hank of Oliver's hair, with tears running down my face. This went on for many months, and even the gift of an Akita puppy did little to assuage my grief, for with Oliver I had known a sense of partnership and communion such as I had rarely known with human beings. Maybe it was his transitional nature that made me love him so: his attempt to imitate other dogs, even other people; his bright, bold, valiant endeavor to be more than the form and species that the Great Dispatcher had given him this time around. Friends would tell me that it was a known fact that you stopped mourning a pet after three months. Not so. Not so at all.

Today I look back at what a wonderful teacher Oliver was with his attempts to try and move past the boundaries of traditional dogdom. My aim in all my work is similar: the discovery and employment of the means to elicit the possible human out of the raw material of our traditional notion of ourselves.

Airedales are much given to all manner of creative endeavors. They are entrepreneurs in dog form, always seeking out new projects, hobbies, and relationships. Saji Jinootsa, my second Airedale, was a petite little lady with elegant manners and a penchant for dressing up. In the "mystery school" that I run on weekends devoted to exploring the psychological and spiritual potentials of people and cultures, I often tell about the lives of great men and women who have contributed much to the advancement of the human race. Saji's role would be to come dressed like these: a tricornered hat and eighteenth-century-type vest for Thomas Jefferson, dark glasses and a shawl for Helen Keller, a sari for Gandhi's wife.

Saji was a great performer. A quick study, she would help enact the scenes of the lives described. She "studied" the various roles she was given, listening carefully to her instructions, seeming to understand the innate dignity of each portrayal. She allowed herself to be dressed in all manner of costumes, be led through scenes, and look inquiringly at whoever was addressing her. In this she was not unlike Wishbone, the remarkable Jack Russell terrier who had his own PBS series playing leading characters in literature, like the Greek war hero and adventurer Odysseus and George Eliot's wrongly accused weaver, Silas Marner. But her favorite performance was that of a beautifully decked out bridesmaid at the weddings at which I occasionally officiated for my students. Solemnly, stately, she would walk down the aisle, giving a stern look to those who giggled uncontrollably at her passing. She would be the first to kiss the bride after the new husband and willingly let her front paws be lifted up to dance on her hind legs with the youngsters at the celebration afterward.

Saji was as persevering in her outdoor life as she was in her indoor one. From puppyhood it was clear that she had been born to swim! At the stroke of noon from April to late October, she would demand to be let out so she could get to our swimming pool. We would throw sticks and she would dive in, retrieve them, and bring them back for us to throw again . . . and again . . . and again. After the thirtieth throw we would hand the stick on to some other willing person, who would throw it until exhausted. But Saji never seemed to tire. And when she had exhausted her human complement, she was known to throw the stick for herself and jump in happily to retrieve it.

Saji was outrageously social. She would always get to know our newest neighbors very well before we would ever meet them. Later in life, she took to taking herself on very long walks to meet new people. Her procedure was always the same. She would bark or scratch at a door, greet the people with great friendliness, enter the living room for a social visit, and then after all amenities had been exchanged, head for the kitchen. There, she would look meaningfully at the refrigerator. Of course, the startled hosts would offer her something from its shelves. After her snack she would find and stand by the telephone, as if to say, "I've enjoyed your company; now it's time for you to get me home." The hosts would read our number on her collar and call us up with the news that we had the friendliest dog in the world. We would pick her up and she would happily return with us in the car, anxious to get in a last swim before supper.

This scene was repeated many times until one day Saji ran out of luck and was hit by a car while crossing the street. She had an exotic funeral attended by her many friends and acquaintances. Her memorial ceremony at the mystery school became a party of celebration in which people spoke beautifully of her social artistry, theatrical skills, and convivial genius.

Saji taught me much about what's possible through her performances, her epic dedication to swimming and fetching, her talent for friendship, and her ability to be part of all occasions regardless of how outlandish. All these were attributes of proving to herself that she could *be* more and she could *do* more. Weariness didn't stop her, for she knew where joy was and was always willing to go for it. Often, when I find myself in some strange city, weary, having to be an academic in front of a university audience, followed by several hours spent working with elderly patients with Alzheimer syndrome, followed the next day by giving seminars on aboriginal cultures to nuns, I think of Saji and know that if she could keep on keeping on, then so can I.

And then there is Zeus, my current Airedale, who is four years old as of this writing. Zeus first arrived in a dream—in fact, a revelation. I was in Cyprus on May 18, 1997, and that night had a dream of a gigantic Airedale, who announced to me in a deep gruff voice, "Hi, my name is Zeus. I'm going to be your Airedale."

Now, we already had two dogs, young Luna, the white German shepherd, and the elderly Akita Barnaby, who was then in his fifteenth year. My husband declared that another dog was out of the question, since two dogs were two dogs, but three dogs were ten dogs. But one day, about a month later, Barnaby walked slowly around the property, visited all his favorite places, kissed each of us, and lay down and died. Some weeks later I picked up at the airport a pup sent by a kennel that specialized in larger Airedales. Looking at his birth certificate, I was not too surprised to find that he had been born on May 18, the night of my dream. Accordingly, I named him Zeus.

Having given my dog an archetypal name, my advice to you is to never do the same, for the name comes with the territory. Zeus, in Greek mythology, hurls the thunderbolts, and our house was hit by lightning several times in one week after the dog was so named, with damages amounting to over six thousand dollars! And it was soon evident that Zeus was going to live up to his name. He grew at godlike speed to become one of the world's largest Airedales—110 pounds of tall, husky Airedale splendor (about twice the size and weight of a normal male Airedale), with the largest set of dog teeth anyone has ever seen. In the winter when we let his hair grow and go shaggy, he looks very much like a buffalo! Zeus holds the opposites, combining softness and extravagant masculinity. Unlike his namesake, he is also the gentlest and most loving of creatures. He has never even growled at anybody—dog or human—and keeps trying to make friends with the deer who inhabit our property. They don't even run from him anymore, but flick their tails and continue to munch away on my vineyard.

Around five months of age, Zeus began to show evidence of radical hip dysplasia. He was one of a litter of three, and his other two brothers had already been put to sleep for a similar problem. His x-rays showed the ball and socket of his hind legs to be a fair distance from each other. Often he was in much pain and tried valiantly to keep up with the noble and sprightly Luna, who soon forgot about trying to get him to leap around with her and gave him many motherly kisses instead.

And yet in spite of all the pain and limitation of movement, Zeus has never complained, focusing his sweetest of natures instead on developing other capacities. Like the blind Italian singer Andrea Bocelli, Zeus has compensated for his disability by becoming, reminiscent of Oliver, a splendid singer. I have only to say, "Sing, Zeus!" and he launches into an operatic rendition that fills the house and much of the property. (Has Oliver been training him from some dog heaven?) In the summer of 2001 the composer and musician Paul Winter visited, and he began to play his saxophone to the resounding hills around my house. Zeus came tearing around the corner, stuck his face inside Paul's sax, and sang the entire piece with him. Never before, said Paul, in all his recordings with whales, wolves, and dolphins, had he ever experienced an animal that would unstintingly sustain a musical duet with him without dropping out and wandering away. There has been discussion of making a CD called "Paul and Zeus."

There have been other compensations, chiefly food. Zeus is a foodaholic and needs to join a twelve-step program for dogs with similar food addictions. Neither wind, nor rain, nor people at the table, nor other dogs in their dishes will stop this giant from what he considers his gainful employment: the seeking out and consuming of all and everything. He mows the lawn with his teeth, strips bark from trees, chews his way through the garden, and is a voracious devourer of anything remotely edible, plus many things that are not.

When Zeus was still a puppy I used to take him to the mystery school, warning my students not to have any food on them and to zip up their purses and bags. This, alas, had little effect, and by the end of the weekend he would be larger than before. Upon arriving home, he would throw up a monstrous variety of things: notebooks, crayons, pieces of shoes, somebody's hat, the dregs of many people's dinners. As it is now, we have to scramble around him after dinner as we try to put the plates into the dishwasher, since he makes it clear that he could do a much better job! He has a capacity not unlike the fabled Diamond Jim Brady, whose every meal bordered on the mythic.

At the age of ten months Zeus had a hip replacement, which has left him virtually cured of his ailment and able to run around in a normal fashion. But in the mornings there is still some soreness and he tells with his body where to massage his hips and how much pressure to apply. He absolutely commands that we be present for him and is a good teacher of what he needs.

In spite of his wild passion for food Zeus likes learning, and even though it involves pieces of biscuit as reward, he valiantly tries to resist his desire to grab the treat from his teacher's hand. It is fascinating to observe his struggle as he rises above his instincts and holds out for more scholarship regarding tricks and good dog behavior. After such a session and even after he's had his treat, he is exhausted from the internal struggle and sleeps for the next hour or three.

Zeus is the doggiest of all my Airedales, so different from Oliver, the transitional dog, and ladylike Saji. But like both of them, he has a magnanimous nature, a can-do attitude, and a character that will never give up and is ever transcending his own givens.

All three of these Airedales, with their expansive natures always trying to overreach themselves, remind me of the stage of the mystic path traditionally called "voices and visions." Here one's "normal" life has been stretched or expanded to include other dimensions of experience, giving one a sense of the possible, of his or her true potential. One perceives with extended senses the magnitude of reality—receiving news from the universe, messages uniquely designed to help one serve the enhancement of both local and universal life. As in my vision quest with Oliver, celestial music is heard—ravishing harmonies, the music of the spheres. Divine words come thundering into one's mind or are dropped in like crystal notes. Strange, sweet aromas, gorgeous tastes, physical sensations of touch, and fire in the belly, in the mind, in the soul are regularly reported by the spiritual adventurer. The world is aflame with the glory of God.

When mystics look within, their inner imagery can match and even exceed their outer perception; in fact, it may be projected outward in so vital a manner as to overwhelm and diminish external realities. From the fertile field of imagination, many mystics like Hildegard of Bingen have created works of philosophy, art, medicine, botany, music, and even statecraft seemingly hundreds of years ahead of their time. They have joined their natural resources to the eternal resources available when their inner mind has opened into universal mind with its infinite treasures.

Like the mystic, we all have the capacity of envisioning, and of imagining and inhabiting, the many mansions of our divine parents' house. Most people, given education and the vision of the possible, can learn to think and feel and know in new ways; function in their bodies with better use and awareness; become more creative and imaginative; and aspire within realistic limits to a much larger awareness, one that is better equipped to deal with the complex challenges of life. Just as Oliver, Saji, and Zeus did with their expanded attunement to the human world, we can step beyond the threshold of our confinement in the objective world and open the gates of consciousness to access the extraordinary realms of inner imaginative space.

This is a breakthrough into higher knowledge experienced by mystics and creative folk who have lifted consciousness so as to perceive supersensible worlds, the original ground of all possibilities. The philosopher Friedrich Nietzsche knew well the revelatory power of this state. In his book *Ecce Homo*, he tells about the nature of his experience of creative inspiration during which he wrote his masterpiece, *Thus Spake Zarathustra,* in three ten-day bursts of inspiration:

> *Provided one has the slightest remnant of superstition left, one can hardly reject completely the idea that one is the mere incarnation or mouthpiece or medium of some almighty power. The notion of revelation described the condition quite simply; by which I mean that something quite convulsive and disturbing suddenly becomes visible and audible with indescribable definiteness and exactness. One hears—one does not seek; one takes—one does not ask who gives: a thought flashes out like lightning, inevitably without hesitation—I have never had any choice about it. . . . Everything occurs without volition, as if in an eruption of freedom, independence, power, and divinity. The spontaneity of the images and similes is most remarkable; one loses all perception of*

what is imagery and simile; everything offers itself as the most immediate, exact, and simple means of expression.[1]

Nietzsche himself says that his Zarathustra work is beyond anything even he could have ever produced—and certainly not in thirty days. He proclaims that one would have to go back millennia, into scriptural times, to find anything similar. In the literature of high-level creativity in art, science, philosophy, and even social artistry, we find similar stories of brilliant work produced from visionary experience. In fact, civilization would still be in its beginnings had it not been for the knowledge and charge given in visions, altered states of consciousness, and interior journeys.

The consciousness that can rise to this occasion needs models of its own matured possibilities, visions of what the possible human can be and do that go beyond the limitations of academic excellence or stubborn persistence to attain certain goals. And I believe that this is true for the animal domain as well. We model some of these possibilities for our dogs, and they strain at the edges of their species consciousness to cross into ways of being that reflect our own. As my dogs demonstrated, they are continually extending themselves just as we are.

And so it is for our perilous time, when everything can be lost within this present century. There is no question that a larger life is latent in the human species and that we live only a small part of the life that is given. For the first time in human history, perhaps, we can begin to live that fuller potential. Beneath the surface crust of ordinary consciousness there lies a world of visions of new possibilities, voices that speak of potential endeavors, ideas, skills, and latent possibilities, all of which are there to be explored and engaged as part of our evolutionary equipment.

If the world is going to continue, it may be that we must rise to the evolutionary requirement and gain intimacy with inner realms, welcoming practical vision and inspiration. This means learning to live on a continuum between the inner and outer—in fact, seeing them as one. This permits us to see things with fresh eyes: we look within to recognize the without, and we look without in order to recognize the within. In this way not only do we overcome set patterns, habits, and conventions, but we are able to strive toward the future as it approaches us. This potential future appears not just as a vision, but as a dynamic, richly felt experience, one that charges us to take those steps to make a better world, both in holding the long-range vision of a possible society and the details of doing the work to help bring it into reality.

The mystic who most serves us as mentor in this regard is William Blake, who was a psychologist of visioning in addition to being a poet, artist, and philosopher. For me, he is the living embodiment of this stage of the mystic path. From his habitation in the realm of voices and visions came strange musics, translucent as well as arcane poetry, auguries, prophecies, paintings and engravings, monsters and angels—the entire citizenry of the visionary life.

Blake was the great original of his or any time. So richly did he inhabit inner space that he could not write a poem without painting a picture or making an engraving to accompany his words. Conversely, so vital were the details of his visions that he could not paint them without providing accompanying words to describe them. His understanding and uses of the imagination prepared the way for the great probings into the unconscious, as well as into the nature of the creative process, that have been made in our time.

Blake regarded human imagination as the essential divine

quality by which Spirit manifests itself in humanity. The truest best life is the imaginative life; in fact, the universe is a creation of the imaginative power of God, which is also present in human-kind. When we begin to realize our imaginative power, we find ourselves on the rich and right path to renewal and creation.

There are few of us who can imitate the range and skill of William Blake. But all of us can accept his invitation to open to a much larger reality. We can sense the creative juices that begin to flow when we decide to live from that greater reality and to push the envelope of our species, as my brave and gallant Airedales—Oliver, Saji, and Zeus—did and continue to do. One of the most important things I have learned from these dogs is to pursue the dream wherever it may take us—they to their adventures and me to my various quests. Too often we have the dream of something that we can do in our life and then let this vision lie about in the backwaters of our mind until it goes dry. But if we persist and, like my Airedales, take on all manner of exceptional tasks, trips, and ventures, then we are filled with energy and courage. We are in-fused with newfound strength, purpose, and clarity.

Many books about dogs reduce them to masses of instincts. (Many books about humans do the same.) But I see them, with their heartful, earnest presence, as teaching us to cross the thresh-old into the next stage of our potential being. Because they love us, they try to become us; because we care about them and the world we share, we too are inspired to stretch beyond our comfort zones and attempt new ways of being. The animals imitate us, and over-reach themselves; they stir us, as do those humans who go beyond themselves stir us. We wake up to the lure of becoming, the strange attractor of the universe; something moves in us that is godlike. It is a consciousness that is not instinctual, has little or no basis in the ancient history of our brains. Rather, this sense of possibility is a call from our future; it comes from our essence and is our divine prerogative. It may take the form of a "voice," in Oliver's and my case, music; a "vision" of expanded possibilities for self or society; or a subtle sensing of aspects of our nature that are as yet unrealized. Whatever the call, it is important to heed its message.

And it is our animals with their energy and drive to keep on growing who can give us the pattern needed to bring our revelation to reality. My dogs have exhibited this behavior in a variety of ways: Oliver and Zeus with their extraordinary singing abilities; Oliver's building endeavors and canine-human romances; Zeus's developing new skills to compensate for a physical defect; Saji's acting the roles of famous people, as well as seeking out new friendships with humans throughout the county. From my Airedales, with their overreaching of expected behavior and pushing their own peculiar envelope of the possible, I have learned much about the possible dog. They have inspired me to seek out the image of the possible human, which I have described in several of my books.

In addition to canine inspiration, I have sought clues to this potential person in many fields—history, literature, anthropology, and psychophysiology, as well as research into the nature of the brain and consciousness. Using various techniques, ancient and modern, and applying the human potentials garnered from my research and travels all over the world, I have guided thousands of research subjects and well over a million seminar participants to redesign themselves as more possible humans.

This is made more feasible by the fact that we are living in a time in which our very nature is in transition. The scope of change is calling forth patterns and potentials that have rarely been needed before. In my work with people in many lands, I have found that things that were once relegated to the unconscious are becoming conscious. Things that belonged to extraordinary experiences of reality are becoming ordinary. And with the harvest of so many different ways of being and doing coming now from the world's cultures, we discover that a larger life is inherent in our species. We, of this time, are pilgrims, pathfinders, and parents of vast new possibilities.

Following, based on findings from my research, is a description of this possible human, a being who I have not yet met in her entirety though I have seen certain of the aspects described below realized in many people and not a few dogs. The first thing that you notice about her is that she enjoys being in her body. A fullness of being inhabits that body, with its flexible joints and muscles, its movements fluid and full of grace. One senses ebullience in the bones, an appetite for celebrating life. She loves the world and sees in every small design—be it plant or flower or rock or smile or simile—the greater design of her Creator. And if her natural zippiness and boundless curiosity entice her into situations where she gets physically hurt, she is able to control any bleeding and accelerate her own healing.

Like the yogi adepts in the Himalayas, she can voluntarily control involuntary physical processes and stay warm in cold weather and cool in hot. (This is true in emotional climates as well as physical ones.) She can also self-regulate skin temperature, blood flow, heart and pulse rates, gastric secretion, and brain waves. Indeed, she can consciously enter into alpha and theta brain-wave states for meditation and creative reverie, drop into delta whenever she wants to go to sleep, and call upon beta waves when she needs to be alert and active. Scanning her body, she self-corrects any function that needs improving.

This possible human celebrates acute senses, which are not limited to five, for she enjoys synesthesia, or cross-sensing, the capacity to hear color and touch the textures of music, capture with her nose the smell of words, and taste the subtlest of feelings. Since her sensory palette is so colorful and wide ranging, she engages and is engaged by the world as artist and mystic, seeing "infinity in a grain of sand and heaven in a wild flower." The splendor of her sensory life graces her with an accompanying gift, an excellent memory, for she is so present to the perceptual richness of everyday life that little is lost or disregarded and all is stored in her memory banks for later review and delectation. She can time-travel into these memories, walk around in them as if they were happening now—talking to this friend, reliving that moment of joy, even holding the hand of a long-ago loved one. Thus she need never feel lonely, for the past is as accessible as the present.

And wherever in the past wounding has occurred, she can visit that time in her mind as the wiser version of her former self and bring understanding, compassion, and wisdom to the occasion. This practice can free capacities that may have been frozen, yielding fruitful consequences for her present and future development. She is, thus, a time player, able to speed up subjective time when she needs it to go faster or slow it down so as to savor lovely moments or have more time to rehearse skills or review projects.

This potential being is a precious demonstration of life in its infinite variety. This is certainly true on the physical plane and unimaginably more so when it comes to experiencing the internal realms. Indeed, the possible human can think in inward imageries and experience subjective realities as strikingly as she can know objective ones. She listens to inward music as complex as any symphony, in fact often richer, for instruments and sounds are added

Chickie and Jean (age 4)
Ready to roll into new adventures of awakening

Titan and Bob
Bob with the Bodhisattva Titan

Zeus
Named for a diety, sings like a star!

Oliver and Bob
Bob bemused by Oliver's brilliance

Zingua and Barnaby
Great Guides to inner space

Jean and her good friend Burton
Egyptian dreaming on a Canadian farm

Nova
Alert to offer grace and service even in the darkest night

Luna
Spirit dog with angel presence

that are unknown to or too arcane for any formal orchestra. She views new movies on her inner screen whenever she wishes, for she knows that it is the nature of the brain to provide stories, well-wrought novels for the inward television station. She uses these imageries to entertain herself as well as to provide the materials of creativity and invention. She is already an adventurer into a vast reservoir of virtual realities and does not need any machine to assist her. She makes use of the fact that self-creating works of art are always budding out of the fields of her mind, and she can capture and rework them as she wishes.

Consciousness for her is a continuum of which she can travel the length and breadth at will. She journeys the inner highways into the United States of Consciousness, entering the state of meditation here, the region of deep prayer there, finding creative ways into the realms of imagination, spelunking her way into the caves of creativity. She continues to discover the many cultures of her psyche and has matriculated in the Innerversity, studying all manner of knowledge and wisdom that these cultures within provide.

She has a deep relationship to the beloved of the soul, the spiritual friend who is her archetypal partner and companion of her depth reality. And daily, regularly, she renews herself in the source places of her soul, where she partakes of the everlasting waters of life and spirit. She lives daily life as a spiritual exercise, and her radiance affects all who meet her for she is deeply empathic, knowing herself as part of a seamless kinship with all living things. Being more, she feels and cares more deeply about the decay and degradation in the social and moral order. In spite of evidence to the contrary, she recognizes the spiritual depth in others and, in whatever way she can, calls them back to their own possible humanity. She is one about whom we might say that "the human heart can go to the lengths of God."

The lengths of God imply the very lineaments and processes of nature and the universe. As I recall Oliver's song on top of the mountain, I realize that in some sense it was a rhapsody to creation and that we are embedded in, if not identical with, this creation. I offer the following metaphor: Our brains are biological stars—that is, energy-burning stars of consciousness—whose systems have a dynamic resemblance to the fusion and fission processes that form and shape our universe. And our thought processes and creativity are the planets around our starry brains. Some of the planets are inert, dead matter that may once have been alive but, through catastrophes like the comets of misfortune or hanging out in the wrong emotional latitudes, have become dust bowls. Others are green and filled with the nutrients of oceanic life.

But the brain could also be seen as a collection of stars as in a galaxy, each neuron standing for each star. Is it not remarkable, then, that there are 200 billion stars in our galaxy and 200 billion neurons in our brains? What's going on here, folks? Are we talking about a unity here, a mind/brain system that mirrors the universe, as it is indeed nested in this universe? Beyond it is a field of being, Something or Someone that provides the lure of all becoming through visions and voices as well as the body of all being, the soul of the brain, the world, the galaxy, the universe.

I suggest, then, that the inner cosmos of our brain/mind system is part and parcel of the outer cosmos of the universe and its system; they cannot be interpreted apart from each other. Since the cosmos is organic rather than mechanical in nature—creative and full of purpose rather than purposeless—we must say that we, along with our animals and other life forms, are the same. When vision allows us to know ourselves as the universe in innovative process, we gain a larger sense of our unique role and destiny in time.

Let me remind you that the nature of the universe being creative, intentional, and unfolding, it is not impossible that, as certain Celtic and other mystics have it, for aeons of time, before you ever came to be born, the dream of you was prepared for. The universe, operating as it does from macrocosm to microcosm over vast stretches time and preparation, may have had you in your fullness gestating in its womb since time out of mind, adding not just genes and genomes, but patterns and possibilities. You may well be a 15-billion-year-long project. As the Irish writer John O'Donohue puts it,

You were sent to a shape of destiny in which you would be able to express the special gift you bring to the world. Sometimes this gift may involve suffering and pain that can neither be accounted for nor explained. There is a unique destiny for each person. Each one of us has something to do here that can be done by no one else. If someone else could fulfill your destiny, then they would be in your place, and you would not be here. It is in the depths of your life that you will discover the invisible necessity that has brought you here. When you begin to decipher this, your gift and giftedness come alive. Your heart quickens and the urgency of living rekindles your creativity.

If you can awaken this sense of destiny, you come into rhythm with your life. You fall out of rhythm when you renege on your potential and talent, when you settle for the mediocre as a refuge from the call. When you lose rhythm, your life becomes wearingly deliberate or anonymously automatic. Rhythm is the secret key to balance and belonging. This will not collapse into false contentment and passivity. It is the rhythm of a dynamic

99

equilibrium, a readiness of spirit, and a poise that is not self-centered. . . . When you are in rhythm with your nature, nothing destructive can touch you. Providence is at one with you; it minds you and brings you to your new horizons. To be spiritual is to be in rhythm.[2]

I can truly say that I learned from my Airedales something of that "readiness of spirit," that "poise that is not self-centered," and above all, a sense of the gifts we contain, which, if acknowledged and pursued, can lead to a vision of the possible and life in the kingdom. If we practice vision, beginning with simple things—imagining the taste of an apple, the look of the sunset, the touch of our dog's ears, the sound of the wind in the trees—and then build on these to even greater imaginings—projects we want to attempt, dreams we want to accomplish—all seen and experienced in ever more vivid imagery, then we have the tools and the passion to over-reach ourselves and, like my Airedales, stop boring God.

CHAPTER FIVE

Zingua and Barnaby: Guides to Inner Space

When our saintly mastiff Titan died, he left a void that we thought no other dog could fill. But several months later another mastiff entered our lives, this one a female, who eventually filled that emptiness with her own unique and strong presence. Zingua, as we named her, was the dog about whom it was said she always did everything right. As a puppy she was exceptionally well behaved, and when she began to go to dog shows, she usually won. She was what is known as a "flyer," a dog that never loses. Not only was she a splendidly built example of the mastiff breed, being perfect in her conformations, but she carried herself with an inner grace and dignity that seemed to convey a remarkable serenity in the midst of the barking, whimpering chaos on the part of all the other dogs and their handlers. The only time she did not win was when Bob went to see her, which made her so nervous and excited that she jumped up (all five feet nine inches of her) on the judges. After that, Bob stayed away and Zingua continued to win—best of breed, even best in show.

Seeing her great golden body striding past a field of yapping miniature breeds, one knew immediately that she was a queen of dogs, Amazon royalty amidst the pygmies. As it turned out, we had aptly named her after the notorious conquering African queen of the seventeenth century, Zingua of Angola. More graceful than Titan had been because of her superb body, she brought lithe and leonine qualities to her every step. In my mind's eye I can still see her prancing in the yard, holding a cow's femur bone in her huge jaws as if it were a small stick.

Zingua assumed a most fascinating as well as valuable role in Bob's and my life. As early as her first year she began to be a great companion and attendant to those journeying to the realms of inner space, a job she took to instinctively. In our work in exploring trance and other states of consciousness, she was always alert to people who were anxious or having a difficult experience and went and stayed with them, often making body contact that soon changed their experience to a positive one.

There was no doubt that Zingua had healing gifts. Some of my husband's psychotherapy patients felt that she was more responsible for the success of their therapy than he was. The sheer powerful presence of a very large benign animal that appears to want the best for you is as potent a therapeutic procedure as one could wish. It is as if the stand-in for Nature herself has come to do one good. One client with schizophrenic tendencies often arrived attended, he claimed, by two hallucinations of men, one walking on either side of him. Zingua would snap at these phantom images but never at the man himself, which he found hilarious and Bob found psychologically intriguing.

Bob began to experiment with this phenomenon by giving hypnotic subjects the suggestion that they hallucinate a companion by their side. Under the hypnotic condition, these people would often "see" the suggested companion—a very common happening in such experiments. What was so different here was the way in which Zingua would always zero in on the conjured companion, never on the real person. She seemed to find these hallucinations unacceptable to her reality base, and she growled at them or bit them away.

I have often wondered why dogs and especially cats will stare intently at something that no one else can see. Is it a spook, a spirit, or even someone's dream that got caught in the ethers? Or maybe animals just are present to many more dimensions than we are and occasionally remind us of the fact by scouting out beings who aren't "physically" there.

Mythic in appearance, Zingua resembled a lioness, and she often appeared to our research subjects in their dreams and trance states with jeweled collars and golden light all around her. In these visions she would function as guide as well as protector, accompanying them to remarkable places. She was reported to having taken these inner-space travelers to ancient Egyptian temples, especially the temple of the lioness-headed, human-bodied goddess Sekhmet, whose three-thousand-year-old statue dominated the room where Bob did his work.

Curiously, the mastiff was bred for thousands of years in Egypt before it was taken to Europe and most notably to Britain, where it became known as the Old English mastiff. Judging by the preponderance of ancient Egyptian imagery that Bob's clients and research subjects always seemed to have around his mastiffs, it would appear that these dogs may carry a resonance of ancient times. Either that or Zingua was so soaked in the atmosphere of Bob's Egyptian proclivities and interests that she wore these images like an ancient fragrance. Like other mastiffs, too, she was unusually telepathic and could be summoned with emotions, such as the feeling "I just love my Zingua," or even with an inner image of her padding over to you.

Mastiffs are wonderful to touch because of their short, soft hair covering a body so muscular and full of vitality. This they allow because they love physical contact. If you sit near a mastiff the dog will likely lean into you, creating the sensation of two walls holding each other up.

Zingua especially liked to be in body contact with Bob and would maintain it for hours if given the opportunity, as when he was watching television late at night. As I travel a very great deal in the course of my work and was often gone for weeks and sometimes months at a time while Zingua was a part of our family, she took on the role of assistant wife. She loved for Bob to talk to her and tell her stories while he sipped his postprandial cognac, and she seemed to listen with unfailingly rapt attention. In this she became devoted to what I have come to think of as tales told by a mystic to his dog while drinking. At night she always slept alongside the bed as if guarding against any kind of intruder, her whalelike snores a sonic assurance that regardless of the hour all was well.

I do not want to suggest that Zingua was all sweetness and light. Like even the holiest and most contemplative of humans, she had her shadow side. It manifested in the fact that Zingua's notion of intruders included not just hallucinations but also other dogs. She was usually the essence of kindness and gentleness to human beings, but those qualities did not extend to her behavior toward dogs, with the exception of our Akita, Barnaby. One time a large German shepherd came over to kiss her on the nose. Bob, watching this scene, thought that for once Zingua was going to be friends with the dog. Then, without apparent rancor or any sign of animosity, she took its head in her mouth and would have crushed it in her huge jaws had Bob not used brute strength to pry them apart and let the terrified shepherd go tearing up the hill.

Zingua also inherited from Titan and Oliver the animosity field between mastiff and Airedale. When the Airedale Saji joined our household, we always had to keep the dogs separate. Saji was a surprise gift from a friend, who delivered her without warning to our door. Zingua met them and promptly tried to swallow the tiny puppy whole without even bothering to chew. Bob thrust his hand down her throat just in time and brought the terrified pup back. He threw this little wet bundle of fur to me, while he hauled the slavering mastiff off somewhere.

Zingua was a dog of the visionary world for many years, assisting people in their exploration of the inner realms. Then, in her twelfth year, she began failing badly. One day she showed every sign of dying and looked as if she were saying, "I'm really sorry, but I've got to go now." Her breathing was labored and she could not get up off the ground. I called our general manager, Fonda Joyce, to tell her that Zingua was dying. "No way—I'm coming over!" insisted Fonda, who was widely known for her force-of-nature personality and Napoleonic will.

A few minutes later, we heard the *click, click, click* of Fonda's high-heeled shoes. She tore into the kitchen, opened the refrigerator, and took out a bag of carrots—Zingua's favorite treat. "Carrots, Zingua," she announced brightly, getting down on the floor next to the ailing dog. "Zingua, you have to live," she repeated over and over again, bringing a carrot closer to Zingua's head. "Eat your carrots and live!"

Zingua's eyes lost their stupor as she took a small bit of carrot from Fonda's hand. Fonda kept luring her with more carrots, insisting that she'd jolly well better stop dying and stand up. After about three carrots, Zingua was able to stand, and we got out her leash and walked her around the property. Fonda, however, collapsed exhausted on the floor, feeling she had given about 70 percent of her life force to Zingua. Indeed, she must have because Zingua lived for some months after that.

It was especially during these last months of her life that Zingua became even more of an inner guide than she had been during her earlier days. Perhaps because she was so close to death herself—had in fact overcome it with carrots—she seemed curiously more capable of helping those sitting near her to descend into interior domains of consciousness. In this, she was not unlike the mythic dogs who accompanied the gods and goddesses who led people into the inner mysteries. "Let's explore the four levels of consciousness, Zingua," I would invite her. Zingua would slowly get up and place her huge head on the knee of the student who was joining me in this research.

In working with interior journeys and other altered states I had discovered a recurrent pattern of "descent" to four levels in the altered-state experience that seemed to correspond to four major levels of the psyche. I came to term these levels the "sensory," the "psychological," the "symbolic," and the "integral," or "spiritual." These four levels of self, four extraordinary worlds, all contain their own treasures and resources. In them lie dormant potentials with which to enhance mind and body as well as to discover one's soul's deepest purpose and, at the spiritual level, to even discover the radiant Source of one's life. Later in this chapter, I will offer a way in which the reader can explore these domains of inner space.

With my research students, however, we had the advantage of Zingua's participation. Her very presence seemed to enhance their journeys, which began by exploring the potent imagery to be found in the sensory realm. Next, in the psychological realm, they discovered levels of personal history and emotions. The third realm of myth and symbol gave them access to the great universal myths and stories that inhabit the human psyche. Finally, in the deepest spiritual realm, they encountered the Great Mysterious out of which we all emerge.

A classic guided tour of inner space led by Bob or myself might find students with eyes closed as they mentally followed Zingua through the four levels. Initially she might lead them to a highly sensate world of dogs and horses, flowing manes, and rich barn odors, then into a country house filled with tastes and smells of gingerbread and chicken soup, with a fire crackling merrily away. Following her from there into the psychological realm, they might discover the members of their inner crew of subpersonalities—healer, lover, artist, clown, maverick, mediator, wild man or woman, saint. Next, in the realm of myth, Zingua might lead them down the yellow brick road or on mighty crusades into strange lands, where they would live out many challenging adventures similar to ones that are found in the archetypal myths and legends. Finally, in the spiritual realm, they would come home to who and what they really were. Journey complete, they would open their eyes to Zingua's great golden body still residing by their side, emanating the contemplative energy that assisted them in going so deep.

Zingua's only friend in the dog world was Barnaby. With him there was no issue of dominance, as he was above all that. An Akita, Barnaby would reveal his Japanese antecedents in his extreme courtesy. He would bow to us in the morning like some Zen monk. And like a monk, he was much given to the peaceful contemplation of nature. Often I would find him looking for many minutes on end at a tree or rock; he had the Zen-like gift of watching the rocks grow.

The Akita is one of the most ancient of all known breeds, and more than two thousand years ago these dogs were raised to be the guardians of Buddhist temples. Perhaps all those centuries spent in quiet and contemplative spaces gave this noble breed its penchant for what can only be described as dog meditation. With his unflappable, peaceful nature, Barnaby was surely the most sweet-tempered dog I have ever known—a mediator between skirmishes of mastiff and Airedale, a compassionate listener, and a friend to all who came through the door. He took everything in, absorbed it all, and transmuted it to serene heartfulness. His presence in a room would calm the energies. Barnaby also had great charm and was exceedingly handsome—people said he looked like a combination of old Hollywood movie stars Clark Gable and Cary Grant. But they also noted an underlying sadness in his eyes, one that was ultimately my fault.

Barnaby had arrived as a gift from my husband about a week after my beloved Airedale Oliver had died. Bob went looking for the longest-living big dog and discovered that Akitas are known to live an average of from fifteen to seventeen years. Unfortunately, I was too broken hearted to claim him as my own, and so in my grieving state I could not bond as I might have with this magnificent puppy. Bob already had his own dog to which he was deeply devoted, the mastiff Zingua. And so Barnaby became everyone's dog, and this added to his sadness, given his penchant for deep relationship. Several of our female assistants entered into profound states of loving communion with him and regretted that they had never found a boyfriend capable of such sweet synergy. Still, I believe that he would have preferred to have been the "chosen" dog beloved of one human. He would look longingly at Bob and Zingua's strong connection, sigh, and place his head down between his paws.

Yet despite his wistfulness, Barnaby's presence seemed to elicit a state of mutual meditation. With him at one's side, one could pass into more peaceful interior states—the monkey mind would quiet, the demands of the day's activities would fade. Many were the times when my associates or I would sit with Barnaby after a stressful day, his paw in ours, and gently pass into a tranquil zone where only peace and stillness abided. Many stories touch us about how important working dogs seem to feel, how good they are at their jobs—herding sheep, picking up papers, monitoring children. Big-hearted Barnaby knew exactly what his work was and did it patiently, without complaint, and with immense kindness.

Barnaby was big in every way. He was capable of long, soulful communication and loved holding hands. He had the Akita quality of actually being able to hold your hand in a humanlike grasp, and when you thought it was time to break it off, he would lift his paw again and take your hand as if to say, "No it's never time to cut connection or to stop loving another person." He was a dynamo of love, generating care, connection, focus, attention, and power. He also offered a kind of gallant courtesy to everyone, being truly a temple dog by breeding and inclination. He was one who embodied the sense of being ever near, and like many big dogs he encouraged deep rest and sweet dreams.

Barnaby was what I would call "heart smart." While other dogs accompanied me on my intellectual journeys and listened while ideas came in, Barnaby just walked and walked with me, looking at the river or the woods and feeling deep feelings. Rarely have I had a walking companion who could just be silent, not having to make a talking point or a barking commentary. With Barnaby, one basked in silence in which much of a more contemplative nature was communicated—peace, simplicity, the glory of the natural world, the presence of God.

The same still sweetness was true, for the most part, in his relationships with other dogs. When Saji entered our lives as a small puppy and was almost swallowed whole by the gigantic Zingua, I took her downstairs immediately to meet Barnaby in an attempt to change her negative imprinting about big dogs. When she saw another huge canine sitting there, she screamed and dropped water. What would this new monster do? But Barnaby merely gazed on her benignly, like a monk momentarily displaced from his meditations. Saji slowly approached and soon began her nonstop game of trying to unfurl his curly tail. Again in monklike fashion Barnaby remained unperturbed, and when he had finished with his "meditations," he turned around and covered her with kisses. He remained her dearest friend in the dog world, a peaceful complement to her social busybodyness.

Like Zingua—and all of us, to one degree or another—Barnaby was of two natures, a higher and a slightly less high. He delighted in running off with Saji and losing her. He would come back eventually, having smelled and harvested the mud in the swamp and gathered every single burr that wanted to travel with him, but he wouldn't have Saji with him. She, being more of a flibbertigibbet and a social butterfly with humans, would cheerfully go on and on until she had no idea of how to get home. Exuding a natural calm, Barnaby seemed to laugh a bit at us for all our rushing around trying to find her. And during the few weeks after Saji's death when he was the only dog in the household, I once saw him in the dining room doing a playful dance, which appeared to be an expression of delight that he finally had everyone to himself. Nevertheless, he welcomed Luna, the new dog that eventually came, with his usual calm courtesy and kindness.

Barnaby maintained this steadfast behavior through the series of dogs that lived with us during his long lifetime until one day late in his life when we got a new, very rambunctious mastiff puppy. By this time he was quite arthritic and had great difficulty standing up and walking. After a day of trying to deal with the pup, he went pleadingly to my husband and as much as told him, "I just can't raise another." Bob understood, and the following day we sent the little mastiff back to her breeder, where she was raised to be a champion among mastiffs.

Barnaby was like a mood, a fragrance of the harmonious inner life, permeating everything with which he came into contact. He knew sorrow and he knew joy, and he held them in a delicate balance of serenity and peace. He knew how to respond equally joyfully to an invitation to walk or talk or sit together, which seems to me to be a particular kind of training in grace—a willingness to respond easily and happily to even the most modest adventure together. Perhaps it could be said that within his framework of being a dog, he lived daily life as a spiritual exercise.

It was on one of our last walks in the woods, with Zingua and Saji now gone and Barnaby getting slower and slower and his hind legs less and less reliable, that my friend and associate Peggy "heard" him say that an Airedale replacement was on the way and that he would be moving on himself soon. Both proved to be true.

The day of his death in his fifteenth year, he visited all his favorite sites on the property and gave them a blessing. Much against my wishes, a hole had been dug earlier that week when the vet had informed us that Barnaby would last only a few days more. In graphic illustration of his Zen-like acceptance of whatever life dealt him, one of his last acts that day was to sit in a meditative state aside the grave, his tail thumping happily in expectation. Indeed, watching him, I was reminded of the Hindu and Buddhist practice of contemplating one's death and meditating in graveyards. Then, slowly, Barnaby got up and walked with me back to the house, made the rounds of everyone present, kissed them, offered his paw, and lay down and passed into another existence.

Both Barnaby and Zingua had remarkable gifts as guides to interior as well as contemplative states of mind. In this, they were representatives of the stage in which the mystic enters a quieter interlude of focus on inner realities—a time of introversion, prayer, or simply entering the silence and being in the Divine Presence. I think of this stage, called "contemplation," as the cultivation of the inner life, during which one uses the resources of spiritual technology to turn inward to meet and receive Reality in its fullness.

Our current historical epoch is unique in that the spiritual technologies at our disposal can be harvested from the whole world: Christian centering prayer, Buddhist mindfulness and visualization, Native American ritual and shamanic practices, Jungian dream work, as well as, for some, the neomystical contemplations of quantum realities. However, whatever discipline is chosen, work and focus are required to make it a continuous factor in one's life. There are many ways to approach this training. All involve reworking the landscapes of the subliminal mind so that there are channels and riverbeds in which a deeper spiritual consciousness can flow. Many people today actively avail themselves of the richness now at hand to organize for themselves a menu of practices that speak to their particular needs and preferences.

With Zingua and Barnaby there were two main routes. Zingua represented the way of images and the muchness of inner space, which in traditional mysticism is referred to as the way of fullness.

This path allows us to extend our perception both to the world without and the world within, the inner and outer senses becoming so refined that we live in multisensory delight, conscious of developing more and more antennae to catch the vastness of Reality. Through heightening our awareness, bringing more and more content into consciousness, and opening to the entire spectrum of emotions, sensations, and ideas, we come to the realization that all things are interdependent and part of the manifested life of the Divine. The technique of exploring the four levels of the psyche helps us to gain access to the multiple realities of our inner world.

I describe this process in some detail in my book *A Passion for the Possible*. Here, however, I offer an abbreviated technique that I often used with Zingua in attendance. To begin, find a quiet place to sit comfortably, and have a writing implement and paper handy. Now select an image, such as a watch or an apple—something simple and concrete—that you will use as the focus for the visualization that follows.

With this image in your mind, imagine that you are entering an underground cave, one that houses the levels of your inner world. Perhaps you can imagine as your guide a dog that you know or have previously known. Go into the cave, then travel downward and inward until you get to a very special door; this is the door to your sensory realm and is highly sensual with silk fabrics and aromatic woods making up its texture. Open the door and pass through, and see what has happened to your object. If, for example you chose a watch, do you now see many different kinds of clocks as I once did? The imagery at this level tends to be highly sensory, a true visionary theater performing for your mind. Its purpose is to allow the richness of your mind's many materials and associations to be released for your entertainment. It also allows for a flowing of imagery that will be needed for the more complex levels to come. Make a mental note of what you see and then write it down.

Closing your eyes again, leave this room and return to the passageway, following your dog guide further inward and deeper until you get to the door of the psychological realm. Sometimes this door appears as a mirror in which one sees oneself reflected at many different stages of one's development. Enter and see what happens to your object here. Once, for example, I took my watch with me and found myself in a realm of crystal balls all aligned around a giant clock. At one o'clock I was a baby, while at two, I was a child. My life progressed developmentally through each of these clock-circling crystals until at twelve o'clock I found myself on my deathbed (with a bevy of folk surrounding me asking me to write introductions to their books before I passed on). I found this vision very helpful in that it showed in such clear if unusual detail the flow of my life. This was especially interesting when I noted that the old lady I was at 11 P.M. was as playful and spontaneous as the child I was at 2 P.M.

You will find that as you become more familiar with this level, memories and associations will surge into consciousness, providing a greater quantity of materials with which to work. These materials could be sifted, analyzed, and ordered to enhance self-knowledge or confront problems in a new way. The visual imagery on this level seems to promote a greater concreteness of thought and also a more than usual flow of imagination and fantasy. This allows for a good deal of creative work. At this level I have seen people map out novels they wanted to write, solve engineering problems, and come up with all sorts of inventions and new ideas. Through my research over the years I've come to realize why this is possible. Since imagery contains a great deal of information coded

114

in symbolic form, there are simply many more patterns of information to use for personal reflection or problem solving. Symbols give us immediate knowledge in visual form that would take reams of words to explain, and they have an emotional impact and clarity that informs the mind as it quickens the spirit.

After recording your experience and understandings, leave the psychological realm and continue with your dog even deeper until you come to the door of the mythic and symbolic realm. This is a door encrusted with symbols and carvings of great mythic folk and legends. Enter and discover what has happened to your object here. It may be that it becomes the focus in a mythic story, which has the effect of bringing you into the adventure as well. I, for example, found myself and my watch in a splendid drama involving Father Time and Mother Eternity, in which Eternity chased Time through many life adventures. Finally, he died and she placed him in a coffin from which he emerged as a baby who suckled at her breast. It was a whole philosophy of time told mythically and gave me much to think about. Be sure to jot down your own particular images of what you experienced here.

What we discover at this level is that we are all encoded with great stories, myths, tales of the hero and heroine's journeys, and even the material of ancient cultures. Zingua's remarkable ability to evoke visionary Egyptian experiences and images was a testament to this great realm of transcendent imagery and stories that each of us contains. This realm seems to be the abode of the archetypal and mythological beings of all times and all cultures. Here, my students often find themselves acting out myths and legends internally and passing through initiations and ritual observances seemingly structured precisely in terms of their own most urgent needs. So vivid can be the experience of living out the life of the mythic figure with whom they are identifying that they report that they have moved into far more profound aspects of their own nature.

Leaving this mythic place, proceed with your dog guide down and down until you reach the deepest level of all, the spiritual realm. This time the door can be a waterfall or maybe even one of fire that does not burn but only purifies. Pass through into the world beyond, where your object becomes illumined as an image of the highest reality; my watch, for example became the moving image of eternity. Often at this level one feels oneself in the presence of God or, if you prefer, the Mind of the Universe. In this realm, images, thoughts, body sensations, and emotions are fused in what is felt as a meaningful process culminating in a sense of self-understanding, self-transformation, spiritual enlightenment, and possibly mystical union. Again record your unique experience.

Beginning your return, pass back through the door of the spiritual realm and, letting your dog lead you, proceed up and up past the doors to the mythic realm, the psychological realm, and lastly the sensory realm. Finally you come to the cave's entrance and leave, patting your dog on the head in thanks for her or his guidance as you emerge into the sunshine.

Reflecting now on the images you have experienced and the notes you have made, see what meaning they may have for your life. With Zingua as guide, people often found that their journeys were not only filled with surprising insights and "revelations" from levels of awareness beneath the surface crust of consciousness, but that they felt safe during the process because of her powerful presence. There is something about the dog as guide into imaginal worlds that gives both safety and validity to the process. Perhaps it is because the dog acts as the familiar, one who is naturally attuned to ways to navigate what have become for us divided and distinguished worlds.

As one practices this process of the four levels and gains some confidence in the journey, it no longer becomes necessary to take an object down. Rather one can take in consciousness some issue or concern, or even enjoy the journey without object or issue, just for itself alone. I have found that bringing an issue as the item of concern into these four realms opens it up to all manner of new perspectives and ideas. Then, too, to journey just for the sheer adventure of it will often offer even stranger rewards, as the unconscious gives one its concerns in technicolor and with potent imagery. Gradually, one learns to live in the remarkable atmosphere of inner space, what is sometimes called the geopsychic realm. Then, like the poet Rumi, one can discover that for every garden in the outer world, there are ten thousand different gardens in the internal world. One has become a citizen in a universe greater than all one's dreams.

This latter approach is closer to the kind of experience that we had with Barnaby. It is another kind of spiritual journey, one belonging more to meditation, in which we retreat progressively from the circumference to the center, clearing the "muchness" to get to the "suchness." Emptying the mind of images and thought, we sink by stages into the great No-thing. Our goal is a pure, imageless apprehension of Reality.

One way of doing this is to get into a comfortable sitting position, close your eyes, and follow your breathing. As you sit in stillness, in a state of peaceful equanimity, find yourself riding the waves of your own breathing. Now picture your mind as a clear blue sky. As thoughts arise, imagine them to be clouds that pass across the sky of your consciousness. Watch them go, but do not become attached to them or follow them. As they pass away, return once more to a gentle focus on the clarity and purity of the blue, cloudless sky. Gradually your consciousness will be only blue sky and, after that, pure consciousness with no object but itself.

As you continue to practice this simple meditation, life's stresses will gradually cease to overwhelm you. Peace of mind and clarity of spirit will become a way of being, as your consciousness and the Mind that is the essence of all Reality come closer together, even into oneness.

In its early practice, this form of contemplation tends to require some of the same effort as learning to read—that is, a conscious changing of focus. Just as, to a child learning to read, the strange and baffling markings on the page gradually become letters, then words, then sentences, then meaning, so in inward-turning contemplation, we discover a whole new way of apprehending Reality that is first glimpsed, then gradually understood, and finally grasped.

What is read ultimately is nothing short of the Absolute itself. As we move from our conditioned existence in the world of becoming to the ground of our existence in the world of being, perceptual assumptions built up by self, need, history, and everyday life dissolve. Eventually, our local lenses become so gossamer as to disappear. The Buddhists call the goal of such contemplation "voidness," or *shunyata;* Christian mystics call it "emptying," or *kenosis.* Face-to-face with the substance of all being, the energy of all creation, we discover to our deep joy that the Absolute has been our essential nature all the time, regardless of how far or how weirdly we have sought it outside ourselves. German mystic Meister Eckhart put it brilliantly when he described the whereness of it by saying, "God is near us, but we are far from Him, God is within, we are without, God is at home, we are the far country."

Barnaby, in his deeply contemplative way, would help me leave behind the usual busyness of my mind and relax into a field of awareness that allowed for sheer dwelling in the Presence. In the same way, for many who might relax with a dog by their side at the end of the day, this is an opportunity for spiritual practice as well. Perhaps the phenomenal growth in the practice of meditation in the West in the past few decades speaks not only to the needs of those who seek relief from overly complex lives and agendas, but also to a breakthrough into the depths, such that spiritual realities are entering more readily into ordinary time.

In this world of almost incessant activity, with so many calls upon one's attention both without as well as within, the threshold to deep mind is at the point of focus. Hindus and Buddhists will often focus on sacred words or mantras, while Christian con-templatives will meditate on one of the attributes of God or even on a verse of Scripture; Islamic mystics will put their attention on one of the names of God or on a sound that evokes certain mental harmonies, as in the Sufi *zikr* practice given in chapter 6.

This focus will gradually diminish the sounds, sights, and thoughts that ordinarily assail one. One moves into reverie and quite possibly into a theta-wave state in the brain. The mind enters into itself; it is the halfway house between the world of appearance and the perception of Reality. One may still feel the pressures and buzz of the outer environment trying to impinge on one's focus, but one refuses to respond or be distracted. As one attends to and builds up one's familiarity and experience in the recollected and meditative states, they gradually cease to be reveries of conscious-ness in a blank field and become windows through which one begins to look out upon the vast spiritual universe. One is aware of an extraordinary spiritual Presence, the Mind of the Maker with all its creative inventiveness. With Barnaby by my side, I would sometimes entertain this state as an exploration of this Mind and the contents it contains, including the essence of many inventors and creators inspired by and now held in this Mind for all time.

As a way of pursuing this possibility of engaging the Mind of the Maker, return to the process of sitting quietly and following your breathing until, again, you ride the waves of breath. Now, instead of a blue sky, imagine a dazzling darkness in which it seems that everything is contained. You have only to think of something and it appears, for you have entered the limitless One Mind. All that has ever been or ever will be is stored forever here.

You sense strange and wonderful energies around you. These are the creator energies, and by knowing them more intimately, you can come closer to your own capacities as a creator. In this sphere you can call upon the energies of the great human creators of all times and their works to infuse you with some of the wisdom and understanding of the Mind that has created everything. A rich and resonant voice invites you to relax into a reverie of imagination. . . .

Continuing to breathe deeply and regularly, scan your body, suggesting to yourself that from your toes up to the top of your head the muscles are relaxing, becoming longer and looser, so that all tension is released and you are prepared to be flooded with new life. Think of your whole body as the realm of pure potential. And having had that thought, release it, and let it just continue in the background of your mind.

You can now align your body with some of the energy of the great creators. Begin with your eyes. Sense them being filled with luminous warmth. Allow them to become suffused with the energy of those great ones who have assisted our own deep seeing into the doorways of the Mind of the Maker.

Who among the world's artists past or present hold that gift of seeing for you? Allow those beings to grace your eyes with a refreshed capacity to see. Perhaps you will want to move your eyes back and forth, as if they were riding waves, and invite Vincent van Gogh's impressionistic ability to see the spiraling waves and ripples of aliveness in the fields, trees, sunflowers, and skies of southern France. Perhaps you will want to stand in the valley at Yosemite National Park in California's Sierra Nevada Mountains and see the rocks and trees as master photographer Ansel Adams saw them, quiet sentinels of creation. . . .

Now pay attention again to your breathing, which is key for the invigorating spirit of invention. Aligning the energy of your breath with the energy of invention, inhale the spirit of the great inventors. Receive the ones who so many millennia ago invented ways of making fire. Feel their incendiary creativeness move in your bones and your sinews. Inhale the spirit of one who discovered the ways of sewing clothes together. Inhale and take in that great inventor who knew how to chip better arrowheads. Inhale those women who found the seeds and began planting them in Neolithic times. Inhale the ones who learned how to tame the animals. Inhale those who put wheels on carts.

And now receive those great inventors whose names are known to us. Leonardo da Vinci, who designed new mechanisms never before thought of. Thomas Edison, who invented something new every day. Eli Whitney, who found a way of creating the cotton gin. Nicholas Tesla, who saw new ways of linking energy and matter. Madame Curie, who discovered radium. Henry Ford and his invention of the assembly line for an inexpensive motor car that increased our mobility. The Wright Brothers and their airplane. Take in this spirit of invention—the minds behind the safety pin,

121

the zipper, indoor plumbing, eyeglasses, and, most recently, the computer.

Now breathe with this inventive energy yourself. Think of something that would make life easier and more pleasant. If you could invent, what might it be? What needs to be made better, more comfortable, more interesting, more outlandish? Dream. Put odd things together. Invent now. The spirit of invention fills you, and you enjoy its play in your mind. . . .

When you finish this process, return to everyday consciousness, and write or draw what you have experienced and discovered. As you practice this further, you will often be delighted at the astonishing creativity of your mind. You will even come to wonder, as so many creative folk have, *Who or what in me is coming up with all this material?*

You will gain a new enthusiasm and respect for the contents of your own creative mind.

With Barnaby by my side, when I did this exercise I encountered a realm that seemed to hold the essence of some of the greatest writers in Earth's history. The inspiration gained there provided me with some of the material of my next several books. Included was a radically different understanding of the nature of the creative genius of Shakespeare, my having sensed something of the essence of this brilliant playwright and poet in one of the special enclaves of the Mind of the Maker.

If you opt to explore further on the journey to the center, return your attention to your breathing and accept that you are living in the Divine Presence. Know that this Presence is the All in All—all there is, all there ever shall be. Practice this daily until you come to that stage known as the "interior silence" or the "prayer of quiet." Here one no longer meditates consciously, but rather surrenders to what Evelyn Underhill refers to as a "stream of an inflowing life, and to the direction of a larger will." In this state one neither thinks nor discusses nor willfully tries to do anything; there is no strain, only a resting in the Presence. It is a turning from doing to being, and there is no longer any separateness. And yet, although awareness of the sensory world is gone, one's awareness of one's own existence remains, but without the previously supporting mental and physical constructs that housed one's existence. This is an experience of what is called by mystics the "quiet desert," the place of emptiness.

Some mystics stay here and you may wish to as well, enjoying the utter emptiness of it all, described as the "dazzling darkness." But for those who choose to follow the meditation practice even deeper, there attends upon it a further stage, in which something fills the emptiness—something unnamable, intangible, omnipresent like sunny air. You need do nothing more but rest in the Presence, knowing that it desires you as much as you desire to be at one with it. Meister Eckhart, who has written as lucidly as any about this stage, says that it is the place where the soul of the human begins to be united with its ground. Minutes or hours might pass in this state, which may feel like an eternal timelessness.

When you feel that the experience is complete, return to everyday consciousness, stretch, and give thanks for the blessings received, then go about your daily tasks with heartful wonder. Some are fortunate to enter these deeper states sooner than others. Some meditate for years and never get much beyond an amiable calm. The point is not to reach a particular level but rather to enter upon and enjoy the journey for itself. There are no merit badges here. Wherever one is on the journey is its own reward.

What, finally, can be said of these types of contemplation?

The self is remade, comes to a new kind of fruition in which faculties that have only been seeds in the deep psyche have blossomed into consciousness. We emerge as another kind of human altogether—serene, creative, and often very playful. We laugh a lot, cry some, and, like Barnaby, have astonishing empathy and a genius for soulful communion. Just as Barnaby, the Zen dog, emerged as another kind of dog, we as humans, become more Barnaby-like in our humanity.

Barnaby and Zingua served as guides to the far reaches of the mind—Zingua into realms of imagination and inner journeys, Barnaby into Spirit Source and places where essence and existence meet and the mystic ways become comfortable and available to everyday life. Both brought special presence and trust. Both led us into the luminous place of consciousness that is ever present, always available. They assisted us in contacting that realm that inspires our daily lives with profound peace and connection with the creative patterns that underlie our existence. To paraphrase one who was deeply connected to this Source, we are such stuff as God is made of, and our little life is part of the Eternal Life. These are the times, ours are the challenges to deepen into this Life so that we may find the sustenance to nurture the next stage of our evolutionary journey.

CHAPTER SIX

Ecstasy and Rapture with Moondog the Miraculous

There he was, grown much too big for his cage, his little bug eyes desperate for connection, knowing that something awful was about to happen—a quick trip to the gas chamber maybe unless . . .

My husband and I had come into the pet store at the Nanuet Mall in Nanuet, New York, looking for Science Diet dog food when we spotted him. The sign under his cage said, "Rare White Boxer." But it also said,

SPECIAL TODAY!

~~$200~~
~~$100~~
~~$50~~
~~$20~~
$10

"Why are you selling a rare white boxer for only ten dollars?" I asked the storeowner.

Immediately the man knew he had spotted a live one. Grabbing me by the elbow he led me over to the cage. "It's because—ha, ha—he is so rare that ordinary people can't appreciate him. Look at him, so friendly, so, uh, earnest, so needing to go to a good home of dog lovers."

The dog looked at me with a yearning I had come to associate only with petitions to the deity. I was the ultimate steak, the answer to all his problems, the beloved of the soul. It was then that I noticed his tongue. It lapped out of his mouth, too long by far, even two times too long than that of a normal dog. His teeth were crookedly and carelessly laid about his gums, his nose looked like the aftermath of a boxing match, and his breathing sounded like that of a car stripping its gears. But there was love in his eyes, and recognition. I was *his*! We were destined to be together.

"Si," added the Hispanic employee, "and if nobody buy to-day, he die tomorrow, right Boss?"

"Well, yes," agreed the boss, "if we can't sell them by the time they are four months old—and he is nearly five months—then we have to have them . . ."

"I get the idea. We'll take him."

The rare white boxer was let out of the cage and danced around me in ecstasy, his little stump of a tail wagging madly. It was then that I noticed that his body had the exact shape of a box and that his private parts seemed to belong to a much larger dog, a Saint Bernard perhaps. I took out a ten dollar bill.

"Oh, no charge," said the storeowner. "For you, no charge at all," he added guiltily.

We arrived home to a mixed reception. "That is the ugliest dog I've ever seen in my life," my secretary declared. "This is a home of beautiful dogs, and he's so . . . awful looking."

Just then our other two dogs came bounding into the room,

having smelled the new arrival. Instantly they declared him *theirs*. To them he was a great beauty, or maybe he just exuded ecstasy and smelled of rapture. You could practically hear them talk.

"He's mine," the Airedale growled.

"No, he is definitely mine," the mastiff rumbled.

"I'm yours, yours, yours!" the rare white boxer sang, bouncing from dog to dog, human to human.

"Well, I guess we could make some money off of him," my husband demurred. "We could bill him as the "World's Ugliest Dog" and rent him to Disney for a series."

When we looked up "white boxer" in the dog compendiums, we found that this curiosity was a throwback to its bulldog origins—the boxer having been bred out of the English bulldog and the mastiff—and that white puppies were almost always destroyed at birth. How "Moondog," for that is what we named him, managed to evade this procedure and end up in a pet shop was a mystery, but then, all his life he had a curious relationship to death.

Take the time he came home from one of his rambles bearing what appeared to be a human leg in his slavering jaws and followed by fourteen of our resident cats. Instantly we urged, "Drop it! Moondog, drop that thing right now!" Further investigation revealed that it was not a plastic mock-up for Halloween as we had hoped, but the real unholy thing. No sooner was it on the ground than the fourteen cats lined up on either side of it, ready for lunch. "Cannibals!" Bob muttered as he gingerly rescued the limb and the police were called.

As this was a Saturday, Rockland County's finest were dragged off of golf courses and ball games, and rushed to our home. The sheriff arrived first, stylish in golfing attire by Abercrombie and Fitch. He poked at the leg with a number-four iron and promptly threw up. More cars arrived and the police poured out, one more shocked than the other by the vision that greeted them. You would think that they had never seen a leg unencumbered by a body before.

The assistant sheriff pulled out his black book. "What is the name of the finder of the leg?" We told him. "M-o-o-n-d-o-g," he repeated as he carefully wrote out the name. Moondog looked up happily at the burgeoning bellies of the growing number of policemen surrounding him.

"Now Moondog," the sheriff addressed him with surprising sincerity and gravity, "where did you find the leg? Take us to the place you found the leg, Moondog." Moondog seemed to understand and immediately took off, followed by a dozen police officers, leading them over hill and dale, through brush, through briar, only to arrive at a piece of Kleenex. We've found it, Chief," one husky gent declared, and a shovel was called for. The ensuing dig discovered nothing but an old bottle cap, and Moondog was entreated to lead them on again. This he did with all the aplomb worthy of that hero of detective fiction Lord Peter Wimsey, police following, Moondog on his part leaving no stone unturned, no tree trunk unwatered. After several hours of this, the police were scattered exhausted on the lawn, the chase forgotten for the moment and Moondog off somewhere on his own. As we were serving them cold drinks, Moondog returned down the hill with yet another human leg in his mouth.

"Moondog!" the sheriff roared. "Where did you find that? Take us there, Moondog. Please!"

Moondog caught the desperation and led the police up the hill to a neighbor's yard. Several recent doggie-pawed mounds of dirt were evident, and the police followed suit in raising more mounds. Many spare parts of the human body were soon uncovered. The police approached the house, gunless and nervous. The bell was rung, all doors were pounded. Nobody answered, but Moondog clearly had another notion. Stumpy tail wagging furiously, froggy jaws laughing and pointing, he led the police into the garage. There, occupying shelves and cases, were still more limbs of human origin. Did Rockland County have the grisliest of mass murderers? Was this the most gruesome find of the century? Visions of front-page coverage by the *Rockland Journal News* or even the *National Enquirer* sped through the minds gathered there. Thoughts of promotion were rampant as were rehearsals of the tale of this find for their relatives for generations to come. Even Moondog knew he was the hero of the day and chased his own almost nonexistent tail to prove it.

Suddenly a car drew up. It was the neighbor and his wife. The police closed in, surrounding the vehicle. A major arrest was about to be made. Did he have a gun? Was he dangerous? The tall, thin bespectacled man who was routed out of the car looked bewildered until he saw Moondog.

"Moondog, have you been digging up my legs again?" he queried. Then, turning to the assembled police, he said, "I can explain. I really can."

"This'd better be good," the arresting policeman warned him.

"Yes, you see, I am a physician, a pathologist really, at Cornell Medical School, and I also teach anatomy and dissection. I needed to get some fresh bones for my classes so I took these arms and legs from the dissection room and buried them in my yard. They lose their flesh faster that way."

"Oh," said the dumbfounded cops, their promotions and dreams of fame evaporating before their eyes. Much vocal abuse was turned on Moondog, who, for his part, went laughing and wagging all the way down the hill to his supper. It had been a good day.

There is a postscript to this story. For several years after this incident one of the policemen would drop in occasionally to spend time with Moondog. The white boxer would greet him happily, and I would find the two of them on the porch, grinning at each other. When I asked the good officer why he so enjoyed Moondog's company, he said, "Whenever I feel down, Moondog just lifts my spirits. I've never met such a happy creature and he makes me laugh. I hope you don't mind."

"Not at all," I replied. "Make yourself right at home . . . with Moondog."

And it's true: Moondog knew the art and practice of happiness, something that we humans often forget or never bother to learn. We dwell in melancholia, thinking sadness is our given lot, and take Ph.D.'s in our own pathology. We inhabit our toxic memories, roil in regret, generally make ourselves miserable, and feel that's what life is about. This gets amplified in our relationships, our professions, certainly our media, and even our national character. This torrent of misery gives us yet more ammunition with which to shoot ourselves in the foot. Altogether, it is a terrible thing, especially since it does not have to be that way at all. However, to remount the slope of negative thought, to be renewed by the renewing of our hearts takes work, and takes observation and imitation of those who know joy and who practice happiness.

Here is where our animals are such prodigious teachers. Moondog woke up happy, his little tag wagging before he opened his eyes. He spent the day in blithe good cheer, and finally, when he lay down for the night, I'd watch his stumpy tail wag slower and slower until he fell fast asleep to dream more joy, more dog happiness.

Then there were his raptures. Suddenly, he'd be seized by joy and roll on his back and kick his legs ecstatically in the air, give several moans of pleasure, then jump up and dance a boxer jig. There didn't seem to be any particular reason for this, just general joy over the fact of living.

Others tell me similar stories about the raptures of their dogs. My friend and associate Peggy Rubin says, "When I walked with my dog Georgie Girl and she would get out ahead of me and I'd call her back, she would turn and race to me, overjoyed to see me again even though we had barely been parted. There was such delight and anticipation of joy in her running toward me—it gave her just another opportunity to express her love of life, of running, of me. Here's another example from her loving life: When she grew old and blind and had to walk with a halter, she nevertheles poured out her immense love for life by running as fast as she could, plowing into snow drifts and falling, or running into things because she could no longer see. But nothing diminished her forward questing, and nothing could stop her from giving life to life with everything she had left to give. It was an all-out total ecstatic engagement with loving the life that she would leave before long."

Moondog was a deviant in more ways than one. A survivor of the first order, he knew exactly how to provoke the rage of our other two dogs and then, slipping out, get them to fight with each other while he guilelessly looked on. He also would spend days on end helping the cats clean themselves, and they exhibited near orgasmic appreciation at the lappings of his foot-long tongue. Occasionally their thrills would give way to scratches, but no matter, since Moondog couldn't feel pain. He would contentedly lick a hot oven, play with a fiery coal that had fallen out of the barbecue, and challenge cars coming into our driveway.

In fact, cars were his passion. He loved to travel, in them or after them, mostly the latter. He had been sideswiped so often that he developed a characteristic limp and a rumbling walk. But he never seemed to get entirely hurt. Except for the day that he chased a truck and caught it. We found him by the side of the road, clearly dying of internal bleeding. Rushing him to the vet, we were advised to immediately put him to sleep, since his inner organs were ruptured.

"Oh, no," I refused. "He will die in my arms, being petted on his way out."

That night as I held the dying Moondog, I watched a "movie of the week" having to do with Mother Seton, the first American saint. The story opened in modern times when an American cardinal went to the Holy Office in Rome to ask that she be canonized. At first, the request was refused, for Mother Elizabeth Seton, an Anglican lady who had become a Catholic sister and the founder of many educational institutions, had had only three verifiable miracles to her credit; full canonization required a fourth. However, the American prelates had provided so much flowing cash to the Vatican that perhaps a special case could be considered? More cash flowed, and America had its first saint. The story then looked back on the estimable life of Mother Seton.

As I watched this inspiring picture, it seemed that the light from our giant screen fell on Moondog's limp and dying form. Finally, when the movie ended, he gave a little weak wag and toddled off to his regular sleeping pillow. It seemed to me that he wanted to die in peace, so I let him sleep.

The next morning, expecting to see a dead dog, I was greeted by an exuberant, leaping Moondog. He ate a huge breakfast, drank deeply from his water bowl, and nosed me to the door, anxious to get out and find some more cars to catch. Instead I gathered him up and took him to the vet. X-rays were taken on the spot and the vet came out of his office astonished. "I've never seen the like," he declared. He's completely healed; it's as if he were never hurt. How could this happen?"

"The fourth miracle of Mother Seton," I announced and proceeded to tell the vet what had occurred. He must have believed me, for the next year he converted to Catholicism.

Needless to say, I immediately wrote to the Holy Office, enclosing a picture of Moondog as well as the veterinarian's before and after reports and x-rays. Maybe it was the photograph of the world's ugliest dog that dissuaded them for I never heard back, and to this day Moondog remains the unacknowledged but verifiable fourth miracle of Mother Seton.

Moondog lived into a ripe old age, engaged in ordinary raptures and day-to-day enjoyments. He passed from this life chasing his tail round and round like a dervish spinning to God, until finally he collapsed and went off to find other ecstasies, other worlds.

Moondog's blissful relationship with life speaks to us of the exultant, joyful state of ecstasy and rapture. In this stage of the mystical path, often after experiencing several levels of deep soul work, the mystic opens ecstatically to meet the Source of all and receive total life, total being. Crossing the boundaries of the local self, one moves into "ex-stasis"—that is, standing outside or beyond the self—and is so flooded and consumed with feeling that one's body and mind expand into rapturous realms. The word *rapture* itself carries with it a powerful sense of being seized, carried off, transported, either physically or mentally, from one sphere of existence to another.

133

Unlike earthly happiness, which comes and goes, the ecstasy of the mystic can continue for a long time, during which one's local mind and local feeling become part of the One Mind, the One Feeling. A Christian might call it the beatitude of paradise. To a Buddhist, it is the "bliss-void." For shamans, it is absorption in the splendor of nature, that rapturous perception at the far edges of consciousness of reality as it really is.

I have been with shamans in Africa, in South America, in India as they drummed themselves into trances of spectacular joy. I have been in Holiness churches in the southern United States and seen people who are taken by rapture shout, clap, and jump with jubilation. In the Ivory Coast, I've observed men and women of all ages—from year-old babies to very old people—praying by doing a chicken-movement kind of dance in which the thoracic cavity is continually flexed and opened up to the beat of the drums to receive the god or goddess. The drumming and dancing allow for the body to become the meeting place for the body and Spirit, and the consequent immersion in ecstasy. Among the dervish Sufis in Turkey, I have watched men spin into ecstatic states wherein they encountered the "Friend," the Divine Beloved, as did their great master, the mystical poet Jalaluddin Rumi, seven centuries before. And I have known an eighty-year-old Catholic nun enter into union with her Lord and for hours be rapt in a state in which her face was radiant with spiritual pleasure.

In ecstasy, the boundaries of consensual reality are crossed, consciousness is altered, and one travels to another realm, living in a bliss that is both here as well as in a greater there. Time is amplified, space seems hyperdimensional, and one knows exceeding happiness. Is this hallucination, or is it, as mystics claim, a more accurate perception of the multidimensional world in which ordinary reality is nested? Real or not, the ecstatic state is natural. The body being essentially hedonistic, the forms of ecstasy are innate and avidly sought. The soul, being geared for happiness, seeks joy in union with the One, for that is the soul's natural home. The mind, too, finds its highest realization, for often one returns from this mystic state utterly filled with knowledge and assurance—not a shred of doubt—about the nature of Reality.

The fifteenth-century Indian ecstatic poet, weaver, and musician Kabir lived his life in rapture. Born a Muslim, he refused all religious distinctions, finding the Supreme Spirit to be beyond all rituals and religious forms. He felt his bones as flutes through which the Divine Beloved played its song. "The flute of the infinite is played without ceasing and its sound is love,"[1] he proclaimed. He celebrated this ecstasy as one who has drunk the "cup of the ineffable," found the "key of mystery," reached the "root of union." Kabir says, "If you merge your life in the Ocean of Life, you will find your life in the Supreme Land of Bliss. What a frenzy of ecstasy there is in every hour."[2]

Kabir knew the great secret, one that many animals know and Moondog repeatedly exemplified: that bliss is the true original state of all sentient beings. We are the Divine in form, and when we remember and tune in to our Source, we are naturally ecstatic. "Look within," he says, "and behold how the moon-beams of that Hidden One shine in you. / There falls the rhythmic beat of life and death: / Rapture wells forth, and all space is radiant with light."[3]

Kabir often experienced ecstasy as being a form of divine music, and in the sixteenth century music was also the mode of spiritual transport for the Hindu mystic Sri Krishna Caitanya. He was much given to ecstatic trances and fits of rapturous frenzy through his performing of a *kirtan,* a form of worship using singing and dancing, which he greatly popularized. To this day, in India, one finds devotees performing *kirtans* for hours—even days—on end, entranced and in a state of spectacular joy. But then, too, one can find a similar look on the faces of those attending theologian Matthew Fox's all night spiritual "raves." As strobe lights pulse to the electronic soundscape, multicultural crowds dance fiercely, and a cascade of projected images tells of the journey of our time: gods and nebulae, creation and destruction, suffering and sacredness.

In so many of the accounts of mystical ecstasy, music and sacred harmonies are mentioned. Perhaps there is, after all, a great music master behind it all. The nature of reality is such that everything is energy, vibration, frequency, and resonance. Even the most solid of material objects is essentially a dance of constantly changing energy patterns. Ultimately it is all rhythm, all music, and, finally, all rapture.

Another explorer of these states, the English scholar Marghanita Laski, in her key study *Ecstasy in Secular and Religious Experience*, reflected on the phenomenon: "An ecstatic experience gave a feeling of being outside time; did this mean that time was illusory and timelessness, perhaps, the reality? An ecstatic experience sometimes felt like translation of a simpler, purer state; was it? Sometimes it felt like a state in which one received new knowledge, wonderful beyond possible rendering into words; was ecstasy perhaps *a foretaste of a next development of man* [italics mine] when knowledge would be wordless and greater? And sometimes ecstasy felt like contact with a transcendental spirit."[4]

Laski's studies and interviews with those who had known elements of mystical ecstasy correspond closely with my observations of Moondog and my own interviews of my students and friends.

136

In each case, we found that nature mysticism played a big part in the experience. Mountains, lakes, trees, spring flowers, light dancing on water, the rising sun, the full moon, the rolling tides of the ocean—these called forth ecstatic moments, surprising joy. Other forms included intimacy and sexual love, childbirth—especially the sight of the new baby—long walks in nature, skiing, and, for me in my salad days, skydiving. Ecstasy in the arts was a major experience, music especially but also dancing, poetry, painting, sculpting, visiting sacred places, and a particularly deep meditation or profound thinking on a subject. This was especially true when some discovery was made or insight realized. States of creative breakthrough were almost invariably described as ecstatic. Suddenly the project or idea pursued fell into place, and one knew the joy of seeing things in a brand new way. Several spoke of the extreme happiness that accompanied their completion of long-term psychotherapy. And some addressed the marvelous moments when they realized that they were not mad, merely mystical!

When asked about physical sensations that accompanied these states, my interviewees greeted me with a cornucopia of sensations: bubbles in the chest, champagne in the toes, fire in the heart, feasting on the air, walking on clouds, tasting heaven. They also cited a sense of intense well-being, an expansion of consciousness, and the feeling of themselves as being in a radiant circle of love that rippled out to everyone and everything, everywhere.

Included in this symphony of ecstatic experience were reports of complete empowerment—one's life regarded as a work of art, so that even the low points are seen as helping toward this consummate revelation. Everything is now seen as possible to accomplish, and one is determined to live in ways that make a better world and bring the divine plan into form. Ecstasy and rapture provide the fuel, the energy, the patterns, the knowledge, and the overwhelming desire to fulfill such divine work. Miracles happen; reality is stood on its head.

Moondog's life was a testament to obvious absurdities, miraculous happenings, and blissful states. Through his unabashed delight in just about everything, he taught me what a *natural* thing this happiness is—natural because we are embedded in the dancing rhythms of cosmic joy. Whether it is running for the sheer doggy glory of it with four feet off the ground, communing with a beloved, or serving those who need our help, happiness and the occasions for happiness are vested in all moments anytime. It is where we choose to put our focus that is important, and too many of us have made a habit of unhappiness rather than seeing the positive in the vicissitudes of our lives.

A lot is known about what activates happiness, even ecstasy. The biology of joy, the emotional chemistry of ecstasy have been somewhat ascertained by scientists looking for the peptides of passion, the molecules of bliss. (More of course seems to be known about the neural triggers of despair and depression.) But all this tends to reduce us to chemical factories and says nothing about the spectacular range of the emotional palette, the mystery of love, the thrill of spiritual experience. Rapture has no exact formula, nor is there a simple biochemical equation for happiness. True, we may have the physiological correlates to these feelings, but their power eludes the microscope and the test tube. I think this is why the philosophy of the mystics is both more pragmatic as well as accurate about the source of happiness and ecstasy. And this is where Moondog's natural instinct for joy has much to teach us.

Let me illustrate by telling of two of the most joyous people I have ever known. Many would say they had little reason to be happy. One was deaf, dumb, and blind by the time she was nine-teen months old, while the other is a man whose country has been stolen and whose culture is dying. Both are mystics and, in spite of their towering intellects, share with Moondog the quality of total openness and warm good humor.

The first person was Helen Keller, the great blind and deaf author, social artist, and helper of so many disenfranchised people. I encountered her when I was eight years old and going to a pro-gressive public school in New York City that believed that children should meet some of the interesting elders of the time. And so our fourth grade class climbed onto the Fifth Avenue bus and went to a private club to meet Helen Keller. I remember being stunned by her radiance. Her eyes saw nothing and yet seemed like beacons of light. Her smile was a beneficence welcoming the world. I had never seen anybody so full of presence and joy in my life, even though I had been exposed throughout childhood to professional comedians who were always laughing (when they weren't sulking). Helen Keller's joy was of another order entirely.

When she began to speak, I heard a voice of strange inflec-tions and cascading notes owing to the fact that she had never heard speech, only felt its timbre with her hand on someone's lips. She spoke to us of the joys of life well lived and of how true happi-ness was not to be attained by self-gratification, but by dedication to a worthy purpose. After she had finished, I was so deeply moved that I knew I had to speak to her. Mind you, I didn't know what I wanted to say, but I knew I had to speak to her nonetheless. When her companion asked if any of us had a question, my classmates squirmed and looked sheepishly at each other. But I found myself raising my hand and going up to her.

Miss Keller placed her entire hand on my face in order to

139

read my question. Her fingers read my expression, while the center of her palm read my lips. Still I did not know what I was going to ask. Her hand did not move from my face. Finally I blurted out what was in my heart: "Why are you so happy?"

She laughed and laughed, laughter rising from another dimension of sound—the laughter of a giant sequoia or a whale. "My child," she said, her voice wandering between octaves, "it is because I live my life each day as if it were my last. And life in all its moments is so full of glory."

Here was a woman who was always available to the radical presence of the present, who in spite of her afflictions and limitations was ever open to the potency of life in all its moments. And as I watched her, unself-conscious, touching faces and hands with such exquisite and loving care, smiling in delight with the children, I knew that I had seen greatness. I went home and told my parents that she was the most alive person I had ever met. Was she physically damaged? Of course. Was she ultimately damaged? Not at all. She had rewoven the remaining filaments of her senses to catch the life beams and follow them wherever they might lead—speaking with children, working with the disabled, helping the marginalized and minority folk who needed a spokesperson. Like Moondog, she lived her life to its fill in the moment.

Now, what would you be like if you took each moment to be a masterpiece of possibility? Suddenly, you are intensely present and alive, connected both with all that is around you but also with the abundance of inner knowledge you contain. Take this moment, if you wish, and regard it as the holy moment, the moment in which everything is right at hand to lead you into joy and discovery. As you practice this, you will find that time itself changes and that eternity and its divine patterns of connection are there for you to enjoy. One enters into a state like that of highly creative people who sometimes do the work of months in minutes, their minds synthesizing, selecting, and choosing because they are not bound any longer by clock time, but by the supreme happiness of creative time. Each day brings new thoughts and feelings, or interesting variations on old ones. Each day brings newness or the deepening of old notions. One wakes up like Moondog and, dare I say it, Helen Keller, filled with anticipation for the adventures of the day. One comes to be living a passionate and often joyous existence.

In my book *A Passion for the Possible*, I observed from my studies of creative people that

> *Many of the so-called larger-than-life people differ from the rest of us chiefly in this respect: It is not that they are actually larger in mind and soul or more brilliant. Rather they are profoundly present to the stuff of their lives, to what is happening within themselves as well as without.*
>
> *They use and enjoy their senses more, inhabit with keen awareness their bodies as well as their minds, explore the world of imagery and imagination, rehearse memories, engage in projects that reinvent the world, are serious about life but laugh at themselves, and seek to empower others as they would be empowered. Quite simply, they are cooking on more burners. And when at last they lie dying, they can say, "Life has been an eminently satisfactory experience."[5]*

I belong to a small group of people who have regular days-long meetings with His Holiness the Dalai Lama. One year we met with him to discuss world problems at his home in Dharmasala, India. In 2001 we met at a retreat center in northern Italy for the better part of a week. Here is a luminous man who bears the tragedy of his people being decimated by the Chinese, who daily faces evidence of the dying of the Tibetan culture, and yet who travels the world preaching his philosophy of universal responsibility, love, compassion, and kindness. When you meet this singular and merry man, you find yourself in the presence of a comic moralist. He giggles and laughs a great deal and is interested in everybody and everything.

We asked him, "Holiness, are you happy?" "Oh yes," he replied. We persisted, "But how can you be happy having lost your country?" "Better to be happy," he replied. "Better to practice joy. I feel better that way!"

When further pressed he told us that he believed that happiness is the goal of existence. We wondered how he, of all people, could think that, given the tragedy of his circumstances. He spoke of the art and practice of happiness. Just like learning a fine skill, he explained, happiness requires the retraining of our mind and spirit as well as our feeling nature and heart. We have to realize how harmful are negative emotions and so must learn how to nourish, cherish, and support our positive emotions.

How, then, can we stop playing the same harsh notes over and over again on the keyboard of our consciousness (in many cases even when the events or circumstances that provoked these negative feelings are long gone or reconciled)? How do we stop feeding what I have come to call the toxic raiders of our minds and instead give nourishment, as the Dalai Lama suggests, to positive memory and thought? I find that it requires us to build up an inner repertoire of positive memory, especially those memories that have strong sensory and emotional power. For example, happy memories from childhood or recent memories of seeing your pet bound about with happiness, holding the hand of a trusting child, celebrating a wedding anniversary, seeing the awakening of insight in the eyes of someone whom you are instructing, meeting a wonderful new friend, reading a great novel in a hot bath on a cold night—you get the picture.

After building such a repertoire, and continuing to add to it, the aim is to anchor these memories in your mind through the repetitive reliving of these so that they can become living memories, virtual realities. The anthropologist Margaret Mead once told me that she was rarely lonely because she could recall positive memory so vividly that she could feel the pressure on her hand of a loved one, even though the memory was more than half a century old!

Again, this is where the "stop technique" mentioned earlier can be helpful. You train yourself to stop when you are in the place of a repetitive negative memory, then replace the memory with a positive thought or memory. It becomes part of your inner flow— a stream of positive ideas and thoughts and memories. Gradually, the quality and emotional tone of your consciousness changes and, like Moondog and the Dalai Lama, you come to live in happiness rather than regret.

Practicing gratitude is essential for happiness. I once asked a woman who is in political life how she could stand so much negative criticism directed at her. She answered simply, "Why, Jean, I just try to remember all the people and things for which I am so grateful, and that gives me both the solace and the courage to continue."

The Dalai Lama speaks of compassion as essential to the art of happiness. The practice of empathy—a deep feeling for another, even positive alignment with the soul and life of another—gives one the capacity for ever growing kindness. And with kindness comes love, and with love comes happiness. These are simple truths, but they are powerfully effective. A further stage lies in opening to God's love, becoming a great receiver. One can even begin to identify with God and God's love in the sense that the theologian and mystic Meister Eckhart affirmed: "If I am to know God directly, I must become completely God, and God I; so that this God and this I become one I."

It is from that place of divine compassion that one sends out blessings and compassion to all beings. This is something that both the Dalai Lama and others who would serve the world perform as a daily practice. And a wonderful thing about this practice is that this goodness comes back to one, multiplied.

What, then, can we say about the ecstatic experience? The problem in the West is that we seem to have lost the skill of spiritual ecstasy. In an attempt to move consciousness to a different bandwidth, we sometimes substitute the excitement of danger and the visceral thrill of bodily peril. To get beyond ourselves, we transgress every boundary of safety, playing at what are now being called X-treme sports—hotdog skiing, hang gliding, canyoning, daredevil skateboarding, stunt skydiving—and engaging in risky recreations—Himalayan climbs, solo balloon sails, party drugs. Or we sit on the couch and watch the new TV shows in which benighted volunteers agree to go through horrible experiences in order to prove themselves "survivors." When we age beyond participation, spectator sports supply collective frenzy—the agonies and ecstasies of the crowd. I've long noted that sporting events have powerful archaic ritual components. Consider football: eleven young heroes carrying the holy egg through the womb of the goalpost, while ersatz virgins dance and scream on the sidelines. No wonder the crowd roars in ecstasy.

There is no question that sex is on many people's minds as a potential route to ecstasy, witness the proliferation of sexual guidance offered everywhere one turns—books, videos, talk shows, the Internet, therapists, and the contents of virtually every popular magazine. And yet the cognoscenti tell us that sexual pleasure in this world is but a pale shadow of the ultimate bliss known to the mystic. In mystical union, one is making love to the whole world. One is no longer other and separate, but one and all others. The sense of union being ecstatic, the bliss exceeds the boundaries of one's previously felt reality. Making love to the whole world . . . that was Moondog all right! There just were no protective walls, no restrictive conditions between him and life, whatever form it might take.

I think of Moondog, whose happiness broke the boundaries of what was possible. His was a literal ex-stasis, breaking the taboos, going beyond the standard-brand reality, busting up the ways that things *should* be. There he was, finding exotic things to exhibit and getting away with it. There he was, getting healed because he was being held and petted under the loving light cast down on his body from the movie of the week about an American saint. He taught us that healing and ecstasy are natural partners. All over the world, right now, someone is being healed by first being inducted into an ecstatic state, whether through prayer, chanting, dancing, or ritual whoop-de-do. Ecstasy reopens our accounts with reality and allows us healings and transformations that belong to a higher order of possibility. Healing and ecstasy tell us that the body and mind always have a different set of rules and seem to obey different laws of form when attuned to spiritual consciousness and reality. Thus the prodigious feats, wild enterprises, and rapid healings that attend the raptures of the mystical or canine renegade. Ecstasy is an evolutionary stimulus that amps us up to higher orders of being.

Most people have had some experience, however brief, of ecstasy. But there are ways of courting it and even learning to stay in these states for longer periods of time. The simplest and perhaps the best is immersion in nature. Being in nature and watching the wind in the trees or the waves rolling in from the ocean or a bird building a nest; observing sunrise or sunset, or the bright energy of a storm—such occasions attune us to our native rapture. The secret here is lack of self-consciousness, which Moondog personified—allowing one's margins to become leaky until one flows into what one is seeing. At the borders of the self is the continent of joy, and to cross that defining place is to enter into bliss. Lying on the earth and letting Earth do its magic can be bliss. We sink into her gracious embrace and become earthed.

This experience of ecstasy can be deeply personal in relationship to the divine person known in many traditions as the Beloved. In our time we are experiencing a rising tide of spiritual eros. This involves the evoking of the Beloved through images that eventually take on so much vitality as to seem as real as our own flesh. We feel filled up by the Beloved. Our bones are flutes through which the Beloved plays the love songs of rapture. In this state, as Rumi tells us, one's heart and mind are so extended by the Beloved, it is as if one perceives the world as it truly is—ecstatic. Through the rapture of this yearning, we come closer to perceiving the great pattern of connections, the primal constructs, the transcendent architecture, the very plans of creation. At this point, in ecstasy, we can only express our heart's fullness in poetry as did Rumi, in service as did Mother Teresa, in providing hope and inspiration to others as did Helen Keller and the Dalai Lama, in helping to lift people's spirits as did Moondog, or in simple acts of everyday help-fulness, as do many of us who thrill to the grace that comes from kindness.

Following is an ancient practice that can help one grow in the state of spiritual loving. It is a form of *zikr* (pronounced "zicker"*),* an Arabic word meaning a kind of exercise or prayer or even discipline that engages consciousness at its very root. Traditionally, this has taken the form of prayers or mantras that become so constant and deep a part of the practitioner's consciousness that one's negative thought patterns are gradually replaced and even destroyed. Best known are the Sanskrit sound "*Om*" or the mantra *"Om mani padma hum";* the continuous repetition of the Arabic name for God, Allah; the Eastern Orthodox prayer of the heart, "Lord Jesus Christ, have mercy on me"; the Greek Orthodox "*Kyrie eleison";* and the jubilant "Alleluia!" The saying of the rosary provides a kind of *zikr*, as do the chants of many Eastern religious groups. All these, however, are predicated upon a specific form of religious belief and worship and would generally not be suitable to one not committed to the understanding and practice of the larger dimensions of this belief, although Westerners have quite successfully been utilizing certain Sanskrit chants with great effect as meditational aids.

The zikr that is presented here is a very ancient one that comes down to us today through the Sufi tradition and provides a practice that does not demand specific religious belief but nonetheless engages by its power and beauty the heart, soul, body, and mind of the practitioner. This zikr is neither a word nor a concept; rather, it is a universal sound made deep in the throat, a hum of communion: "*hmmm . . . hmmm . . . hmmm."* The sound is made three times on each breath and bears with it great psychophysical power. For it is the sound similar to the one made by babies suckling, to

147

sounds of appreciation, of communication, of pleasure of all kinds—gustatory, aesthetic, sexual, and mystical. It is the ultimate approbation, and before its power and beauty the negative thought patterns that plague us seem to dissolve. Once you have learned the zikr, it can be done without this formality in other situations—while driving, while engaged in any and all of life's activities. Care should be taken, however, to practice it formally from time to time, to ground it in its sacred and archetypal form.

To begin, sit in any position that will keep the spine straight. Close your eyes and breathe very deeply, following your breath all the way in and all the way out. As you do this, allow yourself to be filled with peace and light in the inhalation, and in the exhalation to send this peace and light out into the world. Spend from two to five minutes doing this.

In this state, first practice the zikr by inhaling fully and then on the exhalation making the "*hmmm . . . hmmm . . . hmmm*" sound deep in your throat. As you make this sound, feel it as a communion with God or spiritual reality—whatever concept fits your beliefs—and let the sweetness and beauty of this communion continue throughout the zikr. The sound is to be thought of as the resonance and loving communion between you and what you consider to be the essence of reality.

The formal practice consists of a cycle of thirty-three breaths (ninety-nine "*hmmm*'s"). You can keep the count, if you wish, on your fingers, or better yet, get a string of thirty-three beads to hold. At the end of the thirty-three cycles, inhale and hold your breath for a few moments, allowing the sweetness of the communion to move through your entire being as you do so.

When you are finished, in the tradition it is appropriate to acknowledge and give reverence. If you wish, then, bow low, your head approaching the floor, to the God in others. Return. Bow a second time to the God in yourself. Return. Bow a third time to the God That Is. Return. Now sit quietly for a while and meditate in the communion of your experience. Many have told me that this practice builds bliss receptors, for you are joining a physical meditative practice to a spiritual sense of communion with Love or God or your Divine Beloved.

Perhaps the most perfect expression of the ecstatic experience is found in romantic poet William Wordsworth's great lines from "Tintern Abbey":

> *a sense sublime*
> *Of something far more deeply interfused,*
> *Whose dwelling is the light of setting suns,*
> *And the round ocean and the living air,*
> *And the blue sky, and in the mind of man;*
> *A motion and a spirit, that impels*
> *All thinking things, all objects of all thought,*
> *And rolls through all things.*[6]

Dear Mr. Wordsworth, I wish you had known Moondog, for he certainly was one who also rolled ecstatically through all things.

CHAPTER SEVEN

The Dark Night
with Nova

"I was in so much despair, so much pain, but with little Nova in my lap, I feel so much better. She makes me happy. She is such a healing dog."

The one saying these words is Sarah, a woman in the final stages of pancreatic cancer, and Nova is a small tricolor puppy belonging to the Xolo breed (pronounced "sholo"). This little dog is a great friend of mine, and I see her quite often. She looks like a miniature deer, and though many of her kind are hairless, Nova has a lovely coat of silky hair. Her eyes are large and intense in a delicate long-nosed face, on a neck that can extend tall and turn, it seems, in all directions.

For centuries this rare breed, whose official title is Xoloitzcuintli, has been associated with the gods of Mesoamerica and most specifically with healing. In Mexico, among the Aztecs and their predecessor Toltecs as well as the Maya, Olmecs, and others, the mythic dog named Xolotl was soul companion to the fascinating deity Quetzalcoatl, whose name means plumed, or feathered, serpent. This god's story is one of the most powerful and moving myths in the world. One of his quests includes an extended journey to the land of the dead in order to rescue the cast-off bones of humans who lived during a previous age. He performs this difficult adventure with the guidance and help of his holy friend Xolotl. In some versions of the story, Xolotl, the dog/god, is the one who actually finds the bones and brings them back to this world, where they can be used to create a new humanity.

Today a Xolo like Nova is trained to relieve suffering, give hope to our tired bones and bodies, and be ever willing to walk with us through those times that test our souls and try us to the uttermost of our powers. Whenever we are required to spend time in the underworld, experiencing those painful procedures that seem to be essential to our evolving story, this little dog travels with us, showing the way to healing and bringing us to the new day, just as Xolotl in the ancient myth traveled through the dark lands as friend and ally to the god.

Nova belongs to my good friend and colleague Joy Craddick, a physician who has been challenged by cancer and whose medical practice these days consists entirely of counseling cancer patients and making sure that they get the best possible treatment. Joy's own oncologist thought that she needed a medical service dog to boost her immune system as well as help her through the dark night of her long bout with cancer.

Joy knew she had found a special dog when she discovered that Nova was born on the mythic birth date of January 1 of the year 2001 at 1 A.M. Joy learned about the Xolos' work as medical assistance dogs from Dianne Pharo, herself a powerful woman with a luminous smile, whose triumph over ovarian cancer she attributes in part to her two little Xolos, Xena and Star. Dianne feels that their healing power literally saved her life—that Xena and Star chose to be her guardians, thus following an ancient legend that decrees that Xolos select the human they feel called to help bring back to health. These dainty, silken little creatures provide therapeutic care, as Dianne describes it, in this way: "My Xolos heal with their sensitivity to pain, sympathy, love, attention, intention, observation, touch, and unusual radiant heat, which they intuitively direct to my chronic pain."

This powerful body warmth, and the Xolo's intuitive wisdom of how to apply it, was the first thing Joy learned about her new companion. She and Nova had just met and were spending their first night together at Dianne's home, now transformed into a veritable healing temple. Joy mentioned that she needed a hot water bottle to place over her liver; she still felt coldness in that area since having an extensive surgical procedure that included the freezing of her cancerous liver cells. Dianne suggested, "Why don't you let Nova be your hot water bottle?" Joy climbed into bed and Nova immediately jumped up, snuggled under the covers, wrapped her body across Joy's abdomen, and slept peacefully there all night long.

Since then, Nova is rarely out of contact with Joy and travels with her wherever she goes, carried in a special pouch on Joy's chest. The pack reads "Medical Service Dog"; Nova's little head and upper body, front legs placidly crossed, extend out of the pack, while her bright eyes take in everything. She goes to the movies (where she sleeps through everything but the previews, which are much too loud for her); she goes to restaurants (where she also sleeps and never tries to stick her face in the food); and she goes every day to work with Joy in her office, where she greets patients, licks them if they want to be licked, climbs into their laps if that is wanted, and then settles down next to Joy in the chair while she talks to them.

Nova has a nose as well as a genius for finding the parts of her human friends and patients that need healing. She goes directly to those parts and places her warm little body over them. Most patients claim to feel much better emotionally and often physically as a result of her presence. As of this writing Nova is being trained to detect infections and parts of the body that need attention. She is learning how to smell disease in its early stages, even to recognize cancer. She seems to know her job as an immune-system enhancer and also one who accompanies people in their afflictions, making them at least comfortable and sometimes happy. Even patients who normally don't like dogs see her as very special. They say that she makes contact with their souls through the look in her eyes and her cheerful willingness to be completely present for them.

Nova is the kind of dog who helps people through their own dark night of illness and distress. Working with people who for the most part have been given little chance of recovery, she joins her owner in making their last days content and occasionally in helping them get better in spite of their standard-brand medical prognosis. Nova and her mistress, Dr. Joy, give so much loving care that they could be said to be a welcome antidote to current practices of the HMOs.

Joy and Dianne tell me that these little healing dogs know how to release the energies they absorb when working with the very ill. After a session in their native Mexico, they will run outside and find a mud bath to roll around in until they feel refreshed and free again. Nova, realizing that mud baths were limited at Joy's house, devised her own cleansing methods after intense healing work. She would fast and then purge herself by throwing up. Joy and I decided that this might be too hard on her little body, so we began a process of intentional clearing, with hand passes over her body to restore her to her own vigorous health. It seems to work, for she begins eating normally again and becomes her usual picture of vitality and enthusiasm.

In the Aztec myth, Xolotl and Quetzalcoatl carry the dual identity of the evening and morning star, the heavenly body we call the planet Venus. Stories tell how this brave companion supports and encourages Quetzalcoatl during his arduous nightly journey through the underworld so that he may emerge renewed and shining as the morning star. Sometimes he gets caught in the darkness; especially problematic are those long intervals between the planet's last appearance as a dawn star and its return as the evening star. Since the planet is felt to be essential to the well-being of the sun, the dog's steadfast courage in bringing his friend through this deep process is considered vital to the continuation of life on Earth.

Nova follows suit in helping her partner, Dr. Joy, in some of her own spiritual journeys as well. Every week or so, Joy brings Nova with her to my house for a session of healing work. When I open the door, Joy exclaims to her dog, "There's your Jeanie!" whereupon Nova dances madly around before leaping into my arms. From the very start we have had a special relationship; she helps me to help Joy in her pursuit of healing strategies to be found in her own unconscious.

Typically, as I guide Joy into deeper inner realms, Nova herself enters a state of sleep or trance from which she does not stir until Joy returns to a full waking state, having traversed domains of healing energies and images. Often, in these realms, Nova herself appears as companion on the journey, just as Xolotl did for his god/friend. Once, for example, Joy found herself in a temple of all possibilities. There were so many choices that she did not know where to turn or what to explore. Suddenly, little Nova appeared and led her through labyrinthine halls to a room containing many different healing tools to use on her own condition. It was after this session that Joy's tumor decreased in size significantly. Her orthodox physician was surprised, but she, Nova, and I understood the source of her improvement.

Literature, legend, and the media are filled with stories about dogs doing amazing things to save the lives of their owners. They will rush into raging rivers to rescue their drowning masters, leap into fires to pull out a child, bring people back lost in snowstorms or in mountain crevices. Some can sense the onset of dangerous symptoms and will let people know if they are about to have a seizure or a heart attack; many people's lives have been saved with this remarkable instinct. If there is someone to be rescued, found, or helped, many dogs have an instinct that seems to go beyond their training to help, to find, to save. They will do this in impossible or improbable situations, even if it means the loss of their own life.

Thousands of such stories tell us of the wisdom, generosity, and kindness of animals, as well as their ability to sense and know things we do not know and cannot understand how they know. Rupert Sheldrake's wonderful book *Dogs That Know When Their Owners Are Coming Home* is filled with verified accounts of many inspiring animal mysteries. Sheldrake mentions that the evolutionary time line tracing the dog/human story of companionship is now recognized at more than 100,000 years. Between 70,000 and 90,000 years ago, human hunting techniques took a leap forward in effectiveness, perhaps as a result of the training offered to the humans by the wolf-turned-dog!

For thousands of generations human communities utilized the dog's powers as guardian and protector. Wise and attentive

156

people came to regard them as animals with mystical powers, especially because of their ability to keep watch at all hours of the day and night. Bards and sages tell of dogs being the ones who understand the in-between spaces: twilight and crossroads and doorways between life and death. And so, in many ways this mystery continues with the extraordinary number and variety of modern-day stories of dogs as rescuers and protectors.

The terrible events of September 11, 2001, witnessed the tenacious and magnificent efforts of the 350 K-9 rescue dogs from all over the world who labored in the ruins of the World Trade Towers, frantically searching to find people living or dead. In spite of burnt paws, asphyxiation, and other injuries, they persisted in their search. Some of these rescue dogs died in their efforts and are deeply mourned. A friend of mine working at Pier 91, where many of the bereaved and fearful families would go to learn news and/or find a way to visit the site, spoke about the comforting presence of the dogs and cats brought there by their owners to offer furry kindness and warm solace to humans encountering the darkest nights of their lives. On their breaks, the firefighters and rescue workers, too weary for words and too shocked at the hopeless horror of the situation to express their pain, would pet the dogs and hold the cats for a few moments before trudging back to the scene of terror and heartbreak.

One guide dog, who had accompanied her blind owner to his office high in the trade center tower, safely led him down the collapsing stairs to safety. Roselle was a three-year-old Labrador belonging to Michael Hingson. He was working on the seventy-eighth floor of the north tower when the first attack plane struck. Roselle raced over to her master, knowing that something was terribly wrong. Led by her, Hingson made it to the stairway, holding on to her with his left hand while he held the railing with his right. Hingson and the panting dog only stopped briefly for a drink at the twenty-fifth floor, where someone was handing out bottles of water, before proceeding down to daylight and safety. "It's a team effort," Hingson said, a few weeks later. "Roselle and I rely on each other."

Another moving account of dogs and humans traversing the dark night together is a special program that is spreading to prisons all over the country. It began in 1981 when Pauline Quinn, a Dominican nun, set about to establish a "Prison Pet Partnership Program" in Washington State at a maximum-security women's prison. In this program, women inmates learned how to train dogs as well as to develop a profession they could use after they had served their time. Many of the dogs to be trained were themselves rescued from "death row" at animal shelters. Although most of the women had serious criminal backgrounds, many made excellent dog trainers, learning to groom and train the dogs so that they could be put into loving homes. Some of these dogs were also trained to be service dogs for the physically disabled, the elderly, and the blind.

Queenie, a mixed breed, was contracted from a prison program to take care of a young girl who was prone to frequent seizures. In her training Queenie had learned to be seizure alert. She could somehow sense the onset of an attack and would take her young charge by the wrist, guiding her over to rest on a couch minutes before the actual seizure would take hold. Queenie would then place her ear in front of the girl's mouth so that she could tell if the child stopped breathing. Whenever the breathing diminished or stopped, Queenie would give a special bark, which alerted the parents to come and help.

Needless to say, the self-esteem of the prison inmates improves when they see the results of their intense and emotionally charged work in training a special dog like Queenie for someone. The program has expanded into many other prisons, and great numbers of dogs have been saved to enjoy useful and rewarding lives. Actress Ellen Burstyn recently produced a wonderful movie made for television based on this story, entitled "Within These Walls."

At the time of this writing, 100 percent of the inmates in Sister Pauline's programs who have learned to be dog trainers have found employment in this field. And their recidivism rate has been zero. In this way, the pariahs became the preferred, the unwanted the most desired, as imprisoned women and castaway dogs train together to offer special help and companionship.

The rewarding partnership of woman and dog is found in stories and myths from many parts of the world. Pottery pieces dated from 4000 B.C. indicate that the dog accompanied the moon, which was seen as a goddess, and with its boundless energy helped plants grow during the night. We read often of the dogs who served as protectors, guardians, and companions among the gods and goddesses in the land of the dead. The ancient Near Eastern feminine underworld deity Bau is sometimes depicted with a dog's head. Certainly her name sounds like the call my dogs make to greet me when I come home from one of my endless teaching and consulting trips that sometimes feel like the mythic underworld.

Just as the ancient mythic dogs were known as guides through the dark underworld on behalf of humanity, so our present-day canine friends inspire and support us through that stage of the mystic path known in some traditions as the "dark night of the soul." This condition has been described as a spiritual desert: all joy is gone, the Divine Lover is absent, God is hidden, and one feels bereft of every hope. Up to this point, the mystic has had cause for celebration and certainty in the ultimate success of the journey. After so many ecstasies and illuminations, such powerful sights and insights, it seems impossible that one could ever lose contact with spiritual reality or that the wind could so suddenly go out of one's metaphysical sails. But it does. And one is left floating in a stagnant sea, spinning round and round in circles of entropy and the darkness that comes of acute depression.

Yet in this painful stage, which nearly every serious traveler on the road to transformation encounters at some point, are contained the seeds of wholeness and renewal. Historic parts of the self, the final entanglements of habit and shadow, are stripped away. One is literally fired in the flame of night so as to be more available to ultimate realization. The old saying "The night is darkest just before the dawn" has its mystic roots in this understanding.

For those of us following the path of the evolving self, our version of the dark night may be less dramatic, but no less devastating. It seems as if all the good things we have experienced have existed only so they could be lost during this time. Health declines, friends depart, trivia abounds, and every failure, both personal and professional, is amplified. It becomes impossible to concentrate. We feel confused and stupid. We can't understand what anybody says; even the simplest explanations seem clothed in arcane mysteries. Family life becomes the womb of doom. All the faults we ever had loom before us in gargantuan proportions. Nobody likes us, and we gleefully return the favor by disliking and distrusting everybody and everything—sometimes even our own pets. What a disaster!

Let's look at what's going on here, first for the true mystic and then, by way of analogy, for those of us who undergo the dark night in our own equivalent way. In both cases, it is obviously very complex, both physically and psychologically. The nervous system, perhaps exhausted by the demands of previous states of exploration, is demanding a rest. Like breathing, the natural movement of life requires a continuous cycle of expansion followed by contraction, followed by another expansion, and so on. In all the earlier stages of the path, this inner process of expanding and contracting has been understandable, perhaps even subliminal. But now consciousness is saying, "Enough! Shut down for a while!"

Many wise writers describe this period of shutdown in terms of ego death or as the final attempted engulfment of our souls by our shadow material, all that negative residue we have resolutely refused to own. Like the sun blazing forth in splendor just as it sets, so the denied and hidden parts of ourselves rage forth to cut us off absolutely from our fertile depths. We fall into utter darkness, apparently a necessary descent if we wish to continue this journey of self-evolution.

Evelyn Underhill describes this process in graphic terms. She says, "In the stress and anguish of the Night, when it turns back from its vision of the Infinite, to feel again the limitations of the Finite, the self loses the power to Do; and learns to surrender its will to the operation of a larger Life that it may Be."[1]

This means that something profound is happening at depths way below our usual psychological stance. I believe that at such times we are in the hands of the dying and rising powers described in so many of the world's myths and stories. Apparent progress on the outer levels stops so that patterns for the next stage of growth can be woven far beneath surface attention and concerns. We are being re-gestated in the womb of higher possibility. At times like this, it is vital to invite a cherished friend or group of friends to hold the vision of who and what we really are while we wander in the darkness, keeping the faith that we will emerge full of new life and spirit. It is they who affirm to us that in fact something formidable is going on—perhaps the most important event in our whole life. We are being transmuted in the alchemy of God, and all the dross and inappropriate elements are being refined away in the depths beneath conscious awareness.

It is important not to stop the process, or fix the process, or drug ourselves out of the process. And it is very important to know, even if it is below the level of our conscious mind, that like Quetzalcoatl we can claim a spirit companion, a *nahual*, who will accompany us into and through the darkest of times. The Mesoamerican *nahual* is usually an animal. As mentioned earlier, the god Quetzalcoatl found his precious spirit twin in the fearless and determined little dog Xolotl. And while a spirit companion will absolutely serve our soul's needs in such dangerous experiences, the work is done faster and easier when that companion is embodied in a living, breathing, loving animal like Nova, Roselle, and Queenie.

Over and over throughout my lifetime, with its share of personal dark nights (not the mystic's version, only the ordinary, but still dreadful pedestrian kind) my dogs have known not only what my soul has needed, but also that I would survive, even when I felt that I would have a hard time doing so. It is almost as if they have understood and appreciated the re-gestation process going on so far below the outer tears and wounds, and have known how to supply the faith, the warmth, the rapt attention, and the bodily presence that human friends and helpers cannot always provide.

These times of personal disaster and depression can overwhelm us utterly. I, like many of you reading this book, have experienced what most people fear: that we will never recover or make it through to the other side. We believe that huge pieces of ourselves have been lost in the underworld, and we cannot summon the power to believe in a new self. Animals, however, are not afraid of the darker aspects of life and are perfectly happy with us even when we feel broken. After all, they like nothing better than searching for lost things, whether that be a buried bone or a missing part of ourselves.

If we become familiar with all the stages of this holy path of self-evolution, when the dark night comes we will recognize it for what it is and will rest assured that "this, too, shall pass." In fact, it *will* pass and be succeeded by a unitive vision of an entirely new way of living and being. This vision will not necessarily be a pain-free way of sensing the oneness of all things, but it will offer wisdom if we open to it.

For several fortunate years Bob and I enjoyed the presence of a magnificent mastiff that Bob named for the famous explorer and adventurer Captain Sir Richard Francis Burton. Burton's eyes shone with all the luminous power of the Dog Star. (Sirius is said to be the nose of the constellation Canis Major and is the star that reminds me of light even in the darkest night.) He and Bob became joyful companions after the death of Zingua. Bob being a scholar of ancient Egyptian psychological and spiritual traditions, he and Burton would spend many hours together every day contemplating these powerful mysteries.

Burton himself endured a dog's version of the dark night as he developed painful problems with his elbows and suffered operations to ease his pain. But an even more significant dark night occurred in his relationship with Bob. Burton grew to a large-male-mastiff weight of more than 240 pounds, and his connection with Bob was so intense and telepathic that he could sense if people were annoyed at Bob or in any way feeling upset with him. (I believe this capacity to pick up negativity extended to people Bob felt ambiguous about.) At any rate, without apparent outward provocation the normally friendly Burton could suddenly turn on a person and nip her or him.

The third time this happened may have been more the result of his having gone stir crazy: it was during a winter of heavy snows, and he hadn't been able to run around outside as much as he needed. Nevertheless, the behavior was unacceptable and warranted serious concern. I'll never forget the look in those deep brilliant eyes as we loaded him into the station wagon to take him back to the trainer for further lessons. There was so much sorrow, but also an awareness of what he had done and a foreknowledge of the consequences. Within several months, the trainer pretty much gave up on him, partly because he bit one of the workers. Bob and I came to the painful conclusion that we would need to return him to his breeder in Canada. All of us felt heartbroken. I don't think Bob has ever fully recovered from this loss of the magnificent Burton; he still calls it the great failure of his life.

But there was a light, a Dog Star portion of the story, as there almost always is at the end of a dark night of the soul. I became friends with the breeder, a wonderful woman in Ontario named Jean Trudgen. She has become like a sister to me, in that she also feels kin to dogs. She and Burton became the kind of close companions that Bob and Burton had been. And at least once each year as long as he lived, I would trek up to western Ontario to visit the pair, bringing Burton a half dozen hamburgers and a number of very large bones. Jean would tell him the day of my visit that I was coming, and always he would be there waiting at the gate from early morning until I eventually arrived. Then I would spend hours and even several days visiting with him and all the family of Jean's eleven other mastiffs. Burton was the king of this realm, roaming freely through the tall grass with his consort lady mastiffs.

We would take photographs and movies of this adventure back to Bob, but he could never bring himself to consider a visit—the remembrance of the tear was too great. Nevertheless, their communion still existed at some level. Whenever Jean would sit down to meditate, Burton would amble over and put his huge head close to hers. Suddenly her mind would fill with Egyptian images, ideas, and mysteries. Thus, from Bob through the great dog to Jean, a fascination with ancient Egypt!

Though there was a lot of pain in this "dark night" story, the dawn eventually came. Burton's friendship helped light up Jean's life; her friendship helped light up my life; and after Bob's heartbreak at losing Burton came the present light of his life, the angel dog Luna. In the cosmic scheme of things, these periods are part of the process of transformation. If we can remember this when we are going through them, perhaps the pain will be easier to bear. And, if we cannot, it is important, as I said earlier, to have a friend or friends who hold for us the conviction of the light at the end of the tunnel.

If we can believe that the dark nights of our individual souls prepare us for receiving a new vision of life's possibilities, would it be possible to extend that belief to include the planetary story? Certainly we are in a worldwide dark night, with particulars too familiar to all of us to need restatement here. What if, way below our awareness, the planet herself were enduring a potent and anguished (and extended) period of darkness in preparation for a new life for all of us, with a unitive vision encompassing all life in radical partnership? And what if we were to acknowledge our human position as Earth's precious twin, willing to undergo the necessary process to bring this new birth into fulfillment?

What if our primary focus were the art of holding the possibility of a new story for our planet while we in our time suffer this global crisis? We would then encourage one another to break through the invisible bubble of hopelessness that keeps us trapped in the wastelands of our minds. With commitment, passion, and a strong desire to serve, we would support those groups and movements working in real ways to green the wasteland in both inner and outer ecology.

Best of all, we would look at all of Earth's living forms with new and deeply respectful eyes. Those plants and animals who serve us with their lives for our food, those living creatures who walk with us as companions, and those wild ones who live and work their magic beyond our knowing would all be welcomed as brothers and sisters on the path in the great chain of being. Nothing has done more damage to our planet than the human capacity to shut others out from a sense of belonging—be they other Homo sapiens or members of the animal kingdom—and our rapacious need to demand more than we require. If we could open our eyes and hearts to the generous teachings of our animal allies, we might find ways to heal ourselves and abide more tenderly within Earth's embrace.

Following is a meditation with roots in classic mystic practice to assist us in remembering that when we are experiencing a period of great personal trial, we are in truth being cradled in a larger light, the hands of the Divine. But first it may be necessary to release old forms and habits so that we can be rewoven in the loom of heaven to have a finer, more textured self, one that is able to live in the kingdom and breathe its atmosphere. Otherwise it would be like trying to live on Mars without wearing a space suit. You may wish to tape this process, which I am presenting as if I am there guiding you, and record suitable music behind it. Then you can enjoy the meditation with your eyes closed.

To begin, follow your breath all the way in, then all the way out. Continue to do this for several minutes, focusing entirely on your breathing.

Now imagine a place, perhaps one with which you are already familiar, where you are hidden, cut off from the world; maybe it is a cabin in the woods or a house on the beach. Picture yourself resting there for a long time—days, weeks, even months . . . a long time of absolute rest.

Then one day it seems as if you are able to dissolve. This begins with your right arm just dissolving. And not only the arm, but all that has happened in your life with your right arm and hand, releasing and letting go. Now the same with your left hand and your left arm, and all the history associated with them—releasing, dissolving. Your right leg and right foot, along with the experiences they have provided, releasing and dissolving. Now your left leg and left foot—releasing, falling away, dissolving. And your torso, releasing and dissolving. Your neck and throat, releasing and dissolving. Your head and your brain—indeed, all your senses—releasing, dissolving.

Now release your entire history, back through your lifetime. The last decades are gone as if they never happened. Your mature years, released as if they never existed. Your adolescence, vanished as if it never occurred. Your childhood, nonexistent. Your infancy, your birth into life—all have disappeared.

Now, in this state of release, of no-thingness, everything that was you is dissolved. Rest in this no-thingness. You are a speck in infinity that has blotted out. Let it all go. And let go of that letting go, and let go of that, until there's not even a letting go. There is only being itself, the dazzling darkness of utter peace and no-thingness. Rest there for a while in a time out of time, a space out of space.

Gradually something begins to come: a glimmer of loving Presence, vague but familiar. It grows—a burgeoning goodness, a shining in the darkness, a lovingness to you. It is the Beloved, the Godself. It is the Loving One who moves the sun and all the stars. It is, as poet Dylan Thomas described, "the force that through the green fuse drives the flower . . ."[2] The pulse is gentle. The energy is subtle. The loving is deep.

The Beloved is coming home in you. The rapture is sweet, and you are so dissolved that you can be re-solved in love, the profoundest union. Experience this love of the Beloved embracing the no-thingness and filling it with love. There is nothing between you, your soul, and the Beloved. There is only the pulsing wave of love and the subtlest of union.

You are taken into that loving. Your soul is anointed in intimate, everlasting, personal, wondrous love. Receive this boundless love that is intended for you. Know that this love, which is light that endures and empowers, is of you, is for you, is with you. Know yourself deeply, unconditionally loved.

Now, in this crucible of love, feel yourself coming back together, but with your parts remade and strengthened to enable you to live in the transcendent universe. You become cosmically conscious, spiritually at one with the One. So that your history becomes all history. Your joy becomes all joy. Your suffering, all suffering. Your mind, all mind. Your heart, the great heart of the universe. Your soul, the soul of life. Your spirit, the energy that moves the sun, the moon, and the stars, and that moves in you and the tides and the snows and the sap—all life itself. Know that you are not just *part* of the whole, you are also the whole itself.

Your feet begin to feel charged and able to enter the great journey. Your legs are strengthened. Your hands, the great shaping hands that belong to our world as makers, become alive with sensation. The hands with which you love and sculpt and write and dream and draw and embrace and cook and paint and shake—the hands that do so many things—are coming back, empowered now with a superabundant vitality to take on new tasks of courage and compassion.

Now the sensation in your arms returns, strong and supple. Your chest and torso and all your internal systems are made whole in the crucible of love—love moving and enlivening, healing. Your neck and your throat, your lungs and your heart, your reproductive system, your pancreas, your liver, your intestines, your stomach—all are coming back now, returning full of new life. Your face, your mind, your brain, and all your thoughts are enlivened and deepened in this loving. And your spirit is quickened and charged, so that now you know you live in the kingdom right here and right now. Fresh life has been given, new creative powers imparted so that you can be an agent of the divine life in this space and time.

Stretch and feel this life that is love coursing through you. It is a love that is always there for you; a love that overrides the injustices, the sufferings, the wrongs that have been done to you or you have done to others; a love that shines in the darkest darkness like an eternal beacon lighting the way. Know that you are deeply loved and that this knowingness stirs in you, backward into the past and forward into the future.

Now, feel yourself bathing in the sheer delectable goodness of it all. You filled with light, for you are of the light. Sound it if you wish. Sing it forth. Let it move in your lungs and in your voice. Stretch into it. Breathe it. Dance it. Be it. And when you are ready, bring your attention back to your special place and rest there for a few moments.

In the mystic path of the soul's journey through the dark night, one goes beyond self-depreciation to a state of utter surrender to the great movement of Absolute Life. This is the condition for access to the new life. It is the abandonment of old centers of consciousness, perhaps even old centers of brain and nervous system to which we have been habituated for tens of thousands of years. It is the taking on of new centers placed in our holy instrument of body/mind as sacred latencies, whose structures can be attained only through a dieback of the psychophysical habits of millennia. After the dark night these sacred latencies stand revealed, the fruits of the Spirit, enabling one to be a midwife of souls and a parent of new life in others.

I sometimes think whimsically that our planet is known throughout the universe as "Godseed School." This distinction gives us great advantages as well as more than our share of tribulations. Such a school needs sufficient stress to push its students to the understandings they will need in their future role as world makers. One of the main requirements of our world-making course is this dark night, which is giving humans everywhere the opportunity to release old habits and toxicities as they prepare to orchestrate the next stage of biological development and social well-being.

The organizers who run Godseed School have provided us with innumerable diverse companions, allies, and teachers to guide us through the process and encourage us to stay with it even when we feel lost and hopeless. Under the cover of darkness, we are being taught by such as Nova, Roselle, Queenie, and others to trust, individually and collectively, the process of our higher development. I like to believe that the psychological organs we are attempting to grow include those that will create a human version of the abundance of courage, heartfulness, playfulness, and delight that any six-week-old puppy demonstrates so freely.

Imagine the blessing if we could believe that during each dark night of the soul that we endure, and that Earth is enduring now, some steadfast, silken, deep-souled being is holding us the way Dianne Pharo's little Xolos hold her: with a loving amber-eyed gaze that is a healing meditation; with reminders of laughter and the need to rest; with curious delight in meeting others; with devotion and total loyalty; with an uncanny capacity to relieve pain and stress. Maybe these brilliant little dogs can teach us how to sustain ourselves, each other, and the planet through the darkest nights, giving us courage, curiosity, healing, and delight as we await the dawn.

CHAPTER EIGHT

Luna,
Spirit Dog of Union

Among many of the native peoples of the Americas, the beautiful white dog is considered a messenger from God and also a messenger to God, being among the most perfect of creations. Such a one is our long-haired white German shepherd, Luna, who is eight years old at the time of this writing. Hers is a fairly new breed with more than a touch of wolf. They are considered among the most elegant and sensitive of all dogs. And certainly our Luna remains simply the most beautiful dog Bob or I or any of our friends have ever seen. Veterinarians always remark that she is a perfect dog in her conformation—graceful, lithe, and muscular.

Arriving as a four-and-a-half-month-old pup into our eccentric household after several hours on the road, she was at first painfully shy with humans. She had come from a kennel where she had rarely been touched or held. But even from the very beginning she had a wisdom and depth to her eyes. It was almost as if her physical treatment of being basically unsocialized during her first weeks on Earth as well as her wolf inheritance caused her body to be nervous and alert to all possibilities: things could go either way with these human creatures, and she needed to be fervently aware of their inherent instability.

For many months after her arrival Luna sat under the kitchen table and would not relate to anyone except the kind old gentleman Akita, Barnaby. She seemed to exist in another world entirely, and we were but wisps of dreams to her. She would look and look at us, but we could never get close to her. She would not come when we called; we could spend an hour just trying to get her to come inside. This went on for about six months. Even the dog trainer said she would never learn to relate to us. But we thought that perhaps she was simply waiting for some sign that we knew how to relate to her.

One day she inadvertently knocked over a nightstand, upsetting a glass and a lamp. Bob declared, "Luna, it is enough—I can't stand any more of this. You have got to change!" And with that he whacked her on the head with a tray (not too hard; Bob couldn't hurt any animal). In that moment, she became an entirely different dog! She actually grinned up at Bob. He laughs when he describes the scene and says, "She saw the light." She became obedient, didn't hide out anymore, grew eager to be with people. From that day on, she has been Bob's beloved. It was as if Bob had given her his version of *shaktipat*—the *whack* on the head given by Eastern gurus and said to bring on an awakening experience—and it caused her to wake up to who she really is. In actuality, what he may have done is asserted himself as the alpha male of her pack, a language she instinctively understood and for which she had been waiting. Either way, her behavior transformed and Luna began to express her true nature.

Part of her nature seems to be that of a mistress of ritual. Once she came out from under the table, she developed on her own and without anyone's help an elaborate series of ceremonies.

It begins in the morning when she is sure that Bob is awake. Sitting by the side of the bed, she opens her mouth and sticks out her tongue in a very large yawn, at the same time making a sound that she never makes at any other time. It sounds as if she is saying her name and his, "LunaBob," and he repeats it back to her, "LunaBob." Or else she says, "Luna," and he responds, "Bob," in an imitation of her voice.

Greeting established, Luna starts the next phase of her morning ritual. She bathes Bob's feet with her tongue, then sits upon her hind legs and offers first one paw, then both. She curls her paw around his hand, in a clear gesture of holding hands, and they touch noses. After that, he massages her chest and the back of her neck. He runs his hand over the length of her long nose and puts pressure on her third eye, then on the bone at the top of her head, which could be considered her crown chakra. She is absolutely insistent that all of these things be done in order. If any step is left out, she demands that the whole process should be repeated from the beginning.

Once assured that everything is kosher, Luna puts the side of her head against Bob's leg and they walk together to the kitchen. There, she nudges him and walks to the door to the outside to be let out briefly. She quickly returns in order to lead him back to the bedroom to get dressed or to sleep a while longer. This is all done in a way that is very ceremonial and ritualistic. When Bob is ready to go to breakfast, she again puts her body against his legs and moves with him to the door. And their day officially begins.

Of all the dogs we've ever had, Luna is the least doglike. She is not interested in things like chasing sticks, grabbing food, hunting squirrels. She has nothing like Zeus's passion for food, although she enjoys a good appetite. Often she just sits and contemplates, watching things and especially watching Bob. If he is in the kitchen and she is reclining on a chaise lounge on the porch, she follows with her eyes through the window wherever he is moving around the kitchen. Wherever he goes next, her eyes are there ahead of him, for she seems to know where he will be going.

Like Zingua before her, she appears to think of herself as a surrogate wife. Bob says she connects at more levels than most other dogs, her consciousness being more multidimensional and multifaceted than many of the other dogs that we have had. In this she is in direct contrast with her dog companion Zeus, who just amiably clunks along. She seems to be aware of many things at once—relationships to others, her sense of the environment, emotional ambience, and everything that is going on. She has a larger awareness of her whole reality than most dogs and most humans, too. She also seems to be more aware of her whole body in ways the other dogs have not been.

Luna has a gift for unitive experience—for entering into states of union with Bob, with the environment, and, perhaps, with the Presence of the One Reality underlying it all. This gives her certain curious abilities. Bob swears that she can teleport. He walks out of the kitchen, leaving her there, and goes out into the living room. There she sits on the couch, smiling, the corners of her mouth naturally upturned. She maintains her mysterious quality, like a shaman, a spirit dog, a ghost creature able to appear and disappear. When Bob talks to her about her magical powers, she looks at him, winks her eyes, and nods her head. She looks like a miniature horse or unicorn, and is definitely a shapeshifter. When we tie a Halloween unicorn's horn on her head, she looks absolutely at home. Once we attached white wings to her back and they looked a part of her, not as something stuck on. She seemed to feel comfortable with them, as if they were natural to her. And, in a gentle, angelic way, she has a benevolent effect on Bob's blood pressure, which is measured every day. In a before and after experiment, we have found that whenever she comes in to sit with him, his blood pressure goes down at least ten points.

One evening Luna and Bob were watching a television program about angels, when she became unusually excited and alert. Watching her, Bob felt a light go off in his head and he asked her, "Luna, are you an angel?" She jumped up, hugged and kissed him hugely, and waved her long silky tail with utter delight, as if to say, "You've finally figured it out!"

From an early age, she demonstrated her delight in the oneness of all things as we would walk through the woods. Feeling called away to some tantalizing fragrance or activity, nose down, whuffling along the forest path, wolflike, she would pick up news of wonders we could only imagine. "Yes, here's where the deer passed," she would look back at us and seem to say. "A bear went by, a woodchuck, and, oh, the squirrels have been at it all around this trunk!" All that needed to happen to bring her coursing back to us was for her much loved Barnaby to stop and rest his failing body. Like a kindly, ministering angel she would stream back to him, mouthing him in wolf fashion and circling around us all until her pack was ready to move on again.

Of all the dogs I have known, she is the one carrying the deepest mystery, perhaps in part because of her wolf lineage. And perhaps in part because of the angelic aspect of her nature. Whatever it is, Luna is definitely "other." People I know who also have wolf hybrids tell me that they have qualities that are "different" from other "dogs." They most definitely have mysterious qualities that are tapped into some other world. And it may be this very connection to other dimensions or the larger life of nature that gives them their strong sense of personal autonomy. They are free spirits, with their own independent relationship with the universe. They treat their "owners" more as companions, equals, than as their "masters"; they are partners rather than servants. In Luna's case, this difference manifests in the ways she regards us as her comrades, eyeing us with the fond regard that seems to say, "I am bringing you into my world so that you can expand your own."

There is a legend that when we die, the first beings to come out of the land of the dead to welcome us will be our dogs and other pets who have gone before. Bob and I believe that Luna has the power to do that in *this* world, while her humans are still alive. She comes out of her own mystic domain and guides our faltering, benighted selves once more toward the light. Soon after her "conversion" now so long ago, Luna's loving and compassionate awareness expanded to include the entire household, especially anyone in need of special care. Often, when I find myself depressed and weary, she comes over and gives more than comfort. It is as if her magnificent presence and empathic heart lift and guide us beyond our human-bred despair. She appears to have news of the universe more subtle than any I know, and whuffles these soul-spun stories in my ear. My brain waves are sweetened by her charming messages, and I find new mysteries to contemplate.

As Luna and the other dogs I've mentioned in earlier chapters so aptly illustrate, dogs seek union with their owners as humans seek union with God. The intensity of desire for union can inspire us to make the journey, no matter how difficult or strenuous it seems. In other words, the intensity of attraction to the goal is so powerful that it can transcend impossible obstacles, incredible odds.

Love is the key here, and there are many stories of dogs who were separated from their masters but were driven by love to find them across countries and even oceans. Here are several true stories that inspire as they illustrate this point.

An Irish terrier named Prince moved from Ireland to England with his mistress during the early days of World War I, after his master joined the army. There were brief and ecstatic reunions between Prince and his master before Private Brown shipped overseas. Each time the army man left, the dog became sadder and sadder, refusing food, until finally he just disappeared. Ten days followed during which a distraught Mrs. Brown searched and waited. Finally, heartbroken and knowing her news would break her husband's heart as well, Mrs. Brown wrote of Prince's loss to her husband in France.

By the time her letter had reached Private Brown in the mud and trenches at Armentières, the dog had also reached him. Prince had left England, a country he did not know at all, traveled many miles of city streets, trekked across the country to the English Channel, jumped on a boat and somehow made it across the channel, then sped through sixty or seventy miles of France to find one man in an army of half a million Englishmen. Prince did this in the midst of a murderous bombardment, over ground reeking with smoke and tear gas and torn with shells, the air blasting with the sounds of war.

Then there is the story of the dog who stowed away in order to cross the Pacific Ocean. Harold Kildall, second officer aboard one of five cargo ships being loaded in Vancouver Bay, noticed a black-and-white shorthaired terrier. The dog walked cheerfully up the gangplank, investigated every inch of the cargo, and then turned back to shore. Kildall watched while the terrier repeated his careful scrutiny of each of the remaining ships taking on their loads that morning.

The S.S. *Hanley*, Kildall's ship, set sail for Japan at noon. The next morning there was the terrier, resting in front of the captain's cabin—he had stowed away. Soon his knowledge of the ship's routine made it clear to everyone that this was an old sea dog. He kept the watch with the second officer, waited to be fed outside the galley, and slept on a mat provided him near the captain's cabin. He did not respond to the blandishments of the crew, but remained aloof from all, though grateful for the meals, throughout the eighteen-day voyage.

However, with the scent of land, he became alert and watchful. As the ship made its way into Yokohama harbor, the dog grew ever more excited. Other ships also rode at anchor and the dog scanned them each. The closest was unloading the same kind of timber as the *Hanley*'s cargo. The dog focused on it, running over to the rail to be as near to it as possible. Kildall watched as a small Chinese boat drew alongside the next ship and took two men from that ship aboard. As this little boat came close to the *Hanley*, the dog whined and began dancing in excitement, finally breaking out into a loud bark, trying to get the men's attention. Somehow he was noticed, and one of the men jumped up, nearly capsizing the little boat, and began to shout, "Hector, Hector!" waving his arms in welcome. The dog sailed into the water and swam over to the boat. The man pulled him into his arms as they embraced in wild, wet joy.

It turns out that Hector's friend was the second officer of his ship; that's how Hector had known the routine so well. The man had let the dog out for a last run around the dock, and Hector hadn't returned before the tide insisted the ship get under way.

The human being had been frantic and had grieved with his loss; the dog for his part had investigated all available possibilities and found the simplest and most direct route to reunion.[1]

Impossible but true, these tales of dogs seeking and finding union are glorious metaphors for our own human quest across the seas and continents of our own consciousness in search of union with the Beloved Friend at the end of our journey. We may ask, Why do dogs and mystics find their way home? Maybe because in the reality of all there is, our spiritual "Home" is literally everywhere.

My favorite description for this reality is found in a Buddhist teaching story. A clever creator has designed a splendid net (I see it as a huge fishing net), and within each "eye" of the net, each crossing of the threads, is a magnificent jewel. This net is infinite, stretching in all directions everywhere. When one looks at any of the jewels, one can see every other jewel reflected in it. I like to think that touching any jewel also sets the entire net in motion, making incredibly beautiful music. The story is meant to convey what some of the new discoveries in physics also suggest: that reality is an interdependent matrix, the One and the many in an infinite dance. Both dog and mystic can discover the way to the Beloved at any jewel place in the net of reality. They remember what we have forgotten, that everything is right at hand to lead us home.

When I look into our Luna's jewel eyes, I can find reflections of all the dogs I have ever known. I see Chickie and her gracious ways of teaching me to awaken to the splendors of life both visible and invisible. Champ shines there with his can-do attitude that helped me to release the old and embrace the new. There is the bodhisattva Titan, the mastiff whose very presence illumined the minds and spirits of those who met him. There, too, is the brilliant and love-sick Oliver, the gregarious actress Saji, and the comical, ever singing, ever eating Zeus—a trio of Airedales whose voices and visions helped me see the new possibilities there to explore. Looking deeper into her eyes I find Zingua and Barnaby, well placed for theirs were the ways of inward-turning journeys. Deeper still is the rapturous Moondog, with his comical gifts of ecstatic excess. Reflected there, too, is dear Burton, no longer tragic but bounding in green pastures, and little Nova, ever present for those who need healing and cherishing in their dark nights. And, finally, I see Luna herself, the white shepherd spirit dog whose eyes hold the mystery of union and reunion.

Luna's sense of intimate participation with her world and her capacity to lift the heart from the ravages of everyday existence persuade me that she is the perfect canine guide to that stage of the mystic path during which the soul attains union with the One. This is when the Godseed in each of us bursts its shell of culture and habit and blooms into the Godself, which is our destiny. One of the glories of later stages of mystical development is having so expanded an awareness that one is less differentiated from the whole. This state is far above ordinary experience, so intense that it is described as inconceivable, a level of abundant life in which we are one with the heart of creation and the mind of all being. Here we know that, yes, the stars are our destination, but also that the cosmos is within us. Those who attain this state have been called ambassadors to the Absolute, pioneers of humanity, even bodhisattvas, enlightened beings who remain in earthly existence to help the rest of us. And on the canine level, Luna might be seen as such an ambassador.

Evelyn Underhill says that for the mystic the unitive vision creates a new life, "a free and conscious participation in the life of Eternity." One lives in this reality and in transcendent Reality. And one shares, consciously, a sense of belonging, on a deeply personal level, to energies and life far greater than one's own. One experiences "a tightening of the bonds of that companionship which has been growing in intimacy and splendour during the course of the Mystic Way."[2]

Underhill describes three essential marks of the state of union. First is "a complete absorption in the interests of the Infinite, under whatever mode It is apprehended by the self." Second, she tells us, in the unitive life one has "a consciousness of sharing Its strength, acting by Its authority, which results in a complete sense of freedom, an invulnerable serenity, and usually urges the self to some form of heroic effort or creative activity." Finally, the attainment of Union brings with it "the establishment of the self as a 'power for life,' a centre of energy, an actual parent of spiritual vitality in other[s]."[3]

Let us try to understand what these qualities mean for us today. The first mark of union, absorption into the divine life, requires that we evolve to the highest level attainable. Not only must we do our best to recognize and clear away faults and deluded habits of mind (including the painful delusion that we are separate from God), we are also asked to recognize and cultivate all our positive qualities and strengths. This is not the time for debilitating and false humility. Evolution seems to be rescaling us to a higher proportion, in both our individual as well as our collective lives. The mystic path clarifies this process. The local sense of self becomes diminished, and this self is replaced with the divine Self, as the "I" joins the "I Am." In this transformation the local person becomes a universal human.

At the level of social polity, local nations are also transformed. Gradually they become more open to universal means, and the Soul of the World, the mother essence of our planetary life, directs the repositioning of their constituent parts. Is the United Nations, despite all its problems, still the prototype of what will eventually become a planetary society, the global commons as the common good?

The second mark of one who has achieved the state of union is the ability to share in what can only be termed divine powers of effort and creativity. History provides many examples of extraordinary feats accomplished by those who have attained something like this state: Joan of Arc, a simple girl of peasant origins, leaves the sheep she has been tending to lead the armies of France. Saint Francis, a dilettante devoted to his pleasures, does a complete turnabout and changes the spiritual history of Europe. Teresa of Avila, a chronic invalid, breaks with her old way of duty and obedience, leaves her convent, and travels through Spain to change the monastic system. Catherine of Sienna, an illiterate, simple woman, goes into a three-year retreat, emerging from her cell to dominate the politics of Italy. Hildegard of Bingen, who suffers almost constantly with migraine headaches, fights the authorities with almost no one on her side, creates her own order, berates the pope, and still puts forth music, art, and science several hundred years in advance of her time. And, returning to the dog world, Luna, in her own way, has moved beyond the notorious shyness and aloofness of her particular breed to become a radiant spiritual presence and guide.

Each in their unitive state partnered a larger reality and a higher destiny. In similar ways something of the same pattern is happening today in a more secular form in the social sphere. People are responding to the stress of current issues by going beyond themselves. So many are learning skills they never thought to have, often inspired by the "hound of heaven," who woofs at their heels, urging them to tasks they never thought to do.

These folk may not yet be enlightened in the mystic sense, but they are certainly acting as if they were, engaging in enlightened action that is heroic in its creativity. I think of Jerry, who uses his gifts of music and compassion to reach the young new immigrants in inner-city schools; Trish, who helps children with disabilities learn to ride horses as a way of increasing their skills and self-esteem; Dody, who understands the shadows and the glories of the human condition and brings meaning and beauty to those dying in a hospice center. And then I think of Michael and Justine Toms, who in their New Dimensions radio broadcasts seed the world of thought with deeper stories that tell in positive ways the changing of the times. Reaching millions of people weekly and against all financial odds, they offer programs that chart the revolution in consciousness, the landscapes of cultural innovation. Each of them devoted to spiritual practice, they use the insights gained to make a better world.

Finally, the enlightened mystic becomes a power for life and a parent of spiritual vitality in others. Those among us who come to full consciousness of Reality, to quote Underhill, "complete the circle of Being, and return to fertilize those levels of existence from which it sprang."[4] By their very presence, in other words, these enlightened ones, who live simultaneously with us and in other climes, breathing other atmospheres, are dedicated to quickening the Godseeds the rest of us contain, so that we, too, can move into those extended realities.

The mystic path affirms that all of us, as part of our humanity, have the capacity to achieve the serenity and freedom of a unified vision should we choose to pursue it. But this takes a fierce commitment. One does not lose one's innate tendencies or predilections; rather, they are transmuted into their divine form. Those who by their nature are lovers become, like Hindu spiritual guru Ramakrishna or mystical poet Jalaluddin Rumi or spiritual scholar Andrew Harvey, madly in love with God. Those whose passion is knowing the nature of things seek spirit through knowledge, as did Saint Thomas Aquinas or spiritual teacher Vivekenanda or physicist David Bohm. Those dedicated to service, like Mother Teresa, Mahatma Gandhi, eco-philosopher Joanna Macy, and United Nations statesman Robert Muller, become social artists and in service attain the experience of union. Each path results in the subsequent birth of spiritual children of many kinds. As Underhill says,

> *The great unitive mystics are each of them the founders of spiritual families, centres wherefrom radiates new transcendental life. The "flowing light of the Godhead" is focused in them, as in a lens, only that it may pass through them to spread out on every side. So, too, the great creative seers and artists are the parents, not merely of their own immediate works, but also of whole schools of art; whole groups of persons who acquire or inherit their vision of beauty or truth.[5]*

I would add to Underhill's description of the state of union one additional quality. The enlightened ones are in some wonderful way jolly, childlike, playful, funny. They sing, they dance, they roll on the floor with laughter, and they never, ever bore God. That makes them as close to mystical dogs as humans can ever get.

Let us travel back along the corridors of time to meet just

such an extraordinary being. We see a small man wearing a ragged brown robe belted with a rope. His head is tonsured in the style of a brother monk. His eyes are astonishing, for they are eyes like Luna's—deep brown and filled with the light of one who has lived freely within a vision of union with the All in All. He welcomes us to this state, this saint and mystic, this lover of all creatures, great and small. In his lifetime he entered the intense inner space of the unitive vision after an equally intense journey through the mystic path. He therefore illustrates, with his love, the spiritual power the journey contains for anyone seeking to live and love more fully, even those of us who are not saints. This is Francesco Bernadone, or Francis of Assisi, as he is known today, patron saint of ecology and of all animals.

Francis teaches the path through his life story, and he teaches about the path as well. For example, he shows us that it is possible to be in several of the stages at the same time, that some of the stages may be repeated over and over at ever-deepening levels (especially in the early years of one's travel), and that one state can involve a lengthy, ongoing process while other steps are also happening. In other words, the mystic path is not a ladder. Rather, it is perhaps a spiral, or maybe even a doggy journey, one that seems to wander from one dazzling adventure to another only to come home at last and, in T. S. Eliot's phrase, "know the place for the first time."[6]

Only Saint Francis himself could tell us what each stage of the path was like for him, and in fact only he could tell us when each occurred. In other words, it may not be a precisely ordered path, but as I survey his life, I sense this unfolding.

The only son of a wealthy merchant and devout mother, Francis was raised in luxury and privilege. He was the rich kid in town and wore the finest clothes and gave the most elegant parties. Opportunities for "awakening" came in surprising ways. Perhaps the most poignant moment of self-realization for the young Francis occurred when a poor man came into his shop and asked for alms "in the name of God." Francis refused, but then, according to the stories, he thought to himself that if that man had asked for help in the name of some rich noble, he would have given him anything. In a revelatory moment he thought how much more, then, should he give to someone who asked in the name of God? From that time forth his eyes opened more and more to life, and to questions about life.

And yet, even for this mystic-in-the-making, his very human initial response to the call of awakening was to believe that his "deeper life" consisted of becoming a knight and winning battles. Awakening brings with it the sense of being called to fulfill a greater life: there must be something more. What we don't always know, especially when we are very young, is what that something more might be. And so Francis's first such attempt was the ill-fated conflict between the people of Assisi and the aristocrats of Perugia. He rode out to battle filled with martial enthusiasm.

However, instead of experiencing the glories of victory, Francis encountered hideous carnage, and the battle ended in military disaster and ignominious defeat, which left him imprisoned for many long months. Surely this constituted "purgation." Violent fevers shook him, but the time there served only to purify his true nature. Many stories tell us of his sweetness and patience during this time of misery.

"Illumination" came, I believe, when he conquered his phobia against lepers. This occurred when he encountered a leprous beggar on the road. Not only did he dismount from his horse, he reached out to touch the man and kiss his hand, only to have the man disappear and become, for him, the risen Christ. This sustained him ever after, so much so that according to those who were present during his life, he often appeared to live in a state of illumination.

Throughout his spiritual path, Francis received "voices and visions," particularly of his anima figure, La Donna Poverella— Lady Poverty—the beloved of his soul, who appeared again and again and gave him deep teachings about simplicity. It was she who taught him that the way of arms and war was not to be his way. He lived during a time of "joyful bellicosity," yet his message was one of peace. His dream life was also a rich part of his voices and visions, and often provided him with information about his next stage.

Francis entered profound levels of prayer and "contemplation" as he considered the messages he received from sacred powers. During one such time of wandering the hills, he walked into an abandoned church. His meditative question at that time was, "Lord, what do you want me to do?" He looked up to the crudely carved crucifix and felt the answer come from the figure: "Francis, rebuild my church." I am particularly fond of this part of his mission because he took it literally. Certainly the command was filled metaphorically, since Francis and his message did much to help bring new life and higher values to the decaying life of the thirteenth-century Roman Church, but he also went to work with stones and mortar and actually rebuilt the physical building. It became the residence of his most famous convert, Clare, and her sisters.

One of his "mistakes" led him to his greatest moment of "ecstasy and rapture." When he heard Jesus ask him to rebuild the church, he naturally thought of fundraising. (Very modern, our Francis.) He went to his father's shop, stole the richest fabric, took it to the next town, and sold it. Prudently he never spent the money, but left it in the ruins of the church. His father, however, outraged at the eccentric person his son and heir was becoming, accused him of thievery and brought the case to the religious leaders. In front of the whole town of Assisi, Francis' father poured out invective and fury.

Happily, it was possible for Francis to restore the money to his human father. And he then stood before the entire community and, seeing a vision of Lady Poverty before him, declared that he would thereafter refer only to his Father in Heaven as his father. He returned to his physical father all he could, including the clothes he stood in. The ecstatic Francis stood before the world, naked and alone, yet surrounded and blessed by the thing he knew would never forsake him, his Heavenly Father. He went out to the countryside, singing and praising God. Even when robbers beat him, he kept on singing. For me this scene includes elements of rapture, of the dark night, and of utter union.

Perhaps the dark night came in earnest during the latter years of his life, after so much work and inspiration. We hear of it in flashes: during the siege of Damietta among Crusaders when the love of God, for which they claimed to be fighting, was utterly absent; when he was thrown into the sultan's prison and sentenced to die; when his order departed from his rule of poverty and began to accept huge gifts of property; when he entered extended periods of doubt and disillusion.

It is recorded that the most poignant periods were the long dark nights of anguished prayer in the mountain fastness of Averna, thinking himself nothing but a miserable little worm, useless to God and to his fellow humans. It finally came to his fervent wish to have two gifts: the actual experience of the love for all beings that his Christ had and the physical pain that his Christ had endured upon the cross. We hear often about the immediate response to that prayer: a six-winged seraph on a cross blazed out of heaven and seared him with the stigmata on his hands, feet, and side. We see only the results of his answer to the first part of the prayer: a magnification of the love and delight he felt for all beings. He has become legendary for that love.

His love of animals was so great and his sense of kinship with them so complete that every year on his birthday, in many churches around the world, animals of every kind are led down the aisle to be blessed at the altar. And what a sight it is! At the Cathedral of Saint John the Divine in New York City, I have watched elephants, llamas, cockatoos, an iguana, hamsters, rabbits, ducks, chickens, a raven, an ocelot, tiny mice, a rat, parrots, parakeets, and every manner and breed of dog and cat go solemnly down the aisle for their blessing. And what is so astonishing is that each of these creatures moves quietly with no barking, meowing, cawing, or trumpeting. Their voices are quiet, as is their stately manner. They seem to know that this is a sacred occasion and stay focused on the altar and not on each other. Perhaps they see what our dim human eyes cannot—the living, breathing figure of Francis of Assisi waiting to bless them at the altar.

And why not? For, in fact, the stories of his love of creatures persist to this day. He moved worms from the middle of the road and placed them in a grassy place away from danger. In the winter he fed the bees honey and wine to prevent their starvation. Whenever Francis passed a flock of lambs going to slaughter, he sold his cloak and anything he owned to buy them, to save their lives. When he was a boy in Tibet, our present Dalai Lama did the same thing for animals going to be killed for meat.

191

Francis enjoyed talking to and speaking with all manner of living beings—communing with crickets, conversing with snakes. One of his favorite companions was a handsome, talkative crow. And he especially loved the little swallows swirling through the air in their black-and-white habits like little nuns flying wild. Once when he was preaching to the inhabitants of a town, the swallows sang so lustily in response that they drowned out his words. Finally, he stopped his sermon to the people and began to preach to the birds. In his legendary sermon he told them how much the Creator loved them, having given them beautiful and warm plumage, springs from which to drink, the high mountains and the hills, the rocks and the crags as refuges as well as the lofty trees in which to build their nests. He exhorted them to always sing out their praises of God and the glory of creation.

Once Francis held a song festival with a nightingale. He was renowned for the beauty of his singing voice. As the story is told, first the bird came and sang its heart out. This inspired Francis, so he sang the song of his soul while the bird listened attentively. The bird then sang again, even more sweetly, while Francis listened again, enraptured. Finally the saint sang words of ecstatic joy in the goodness and beauty of life in the Spirit. This thrilled the bird, and the two of them decided to sing together.

Francis saw the fun, the play, the joy, the nobility, the beauty of all living things. He seemed to realize that they spoke a common spiritual language. And when we suspend our attachments to words meaning things, then we, too, can hear music in the wind, "tongues in trees, books in the running brooks, sermons in stone and good in everything," as Shakespeare in his play *As You Like It* challenges us to do. There are many stories about other mystics entering into profound communion with animals, birds, and plants. When one knows the mystic oneness of it all, then the nature within us can respond in loving resonance to nature without. I can no longer look at another person or at a dog, for example, and make a simple judgment, "That's *just* a woman or that's *just* a dog." Instead, our looking at each other becomes a flow of heart knowing and a sense of deep connection and communion between all things.

When Francis of Assisi attained the unitive vision, he reached a stage of being able to love everything and to fear nothing, even wild animals. The most famous of his encounters with dangerous creatures is his meeting with the fierce wolf of Gubbio. This was a vicious and hungry animal willing to attack and eat anyone daring to venture outside the city walls. I especially love this story because it always makes me think of the wolf's closest relations, our dearly beloved domesticated dog companions.

Despite the rampant fear around him, Francis decided to go out and meet the wolf. The townspeople protested, but Francis declared that his faith embraced a power that honored and understood all living things. He took with him his favorite human companion, Brother Illuminato. A few townspeople followed bravely, but they hid in the trees to witness the meeting between the holy man and the wolf.

Seeing them, the ferocious wolf came loping toward what he was sure would make a delicious dinner. Francis just stood there, smiling. He made the sign of the cross and allowed the power of the Holy Spirit to fill him completely. The wolf slowed down, then stopped. Francis began to speak. "Brother Wolf, come over here to me. In the name of Christ I order you not to hurt me or anyone else." The big wolf ambled over and lay down like a lamb. "Brother Wolf," he went on, "you know you've done terrible things and everybody is your enemy. I know you're very hungry. But you mustn't try and eat people any more. Can you understand me? I want to make peace between you and them, so that they will not be harmed by you any more, and after they have forgiven you all your past crimes, they will not pursue you." The big wolf showed by the wag of his tail and the nod of his head that he understood and agreed.

"Give me your paw to show me that you really understand," Francis exhorted. "I'm going to make a covenant with you. My covenant is that everybody will feed you so you will never go hungry again. Everybody will take care of you and you will help protect the town. Will you promise me that?" The legends tell us that the two shook hands, then strolled back into the town, where, to the amazement of the people, Francis and the wolf repeated their pledge, the wolf again putting his paw in the man's hand.

After that, everybody participated in the care and feeding of the wolf. Each day he would make his rounds, collecting food from door to door. Sometimes he allowed the children to ride on his back. He became the protector of the town. The wolf lived two more years and when he died, all the townspeople attended his funeral.[7]

There is an interesting postscript to this story. Some years ago, during an archaeological excavation in the medieval cemetery of Gubbio, scientists discovered the bones of a giant wolf, which had apparently been buried with great celebration and fond remembrances.

Saint Francis continues to speak to us down the centuries, helping us to be present to the wisdom and simplicity of the animals. May we, too, find that sweetness of spirit to do the same, honoring and learning from all creatures.

Saint Francis loved animals and saw them as members of God's most holy plan, and unlike some animal lovers I have known, he also cared profoundly for human beings. My favorite of his sermons to people begins with the words, "My friends, I wish to send you all to Paradise!"

My wish is simpler. My wish is that we recognize the elements of Paradise that are present on this exquisite Earth and honor them. My work on this book, and listening to the beautiful stories of human beings and the wondrous animals that have touched and blessed their lives, have persuaded me—again—that Paradise is real and possible here. I assume that you who are reading this book and have gotten this far are also close to dogs, fall easily into their eyes, and spontaneously give a smile of pleasure when you see them. I suspect that more than a few of you feel yourself to be strongly kin to them, these cousins on four legs, your very interesting relatives. Perhaps one is sitting by your side right now. Reach over and acknowledge your companion and the journey you share together.

A very great writer and spiritual adept, the Episcopal priest Matthew Fox, once told an audience that his spiritual advisor was his dog. Throughout my life, I have felt the same, even though I have been blessed in knowing and studying with brilliant and wise human spiritual teachers. Yet with dogs, words and theologies are not necessary. With them, you can actually pat and caress the living presence of the Most Holy. You can run and play and dance with spiritual company. You can enter into sacred silence and have even that enhanced by the simple but profound presence of your animal companions. Above all, disabled and often blind and deaf to our spiritual possibilities, we have been gifted with these guides through our darkness, guides to our greater journey. Trust your dogs, for they know the way to the ordinary, extraordinary life in the kingdom.

EPILOGUE

Dingo Dreaming

Several years ago, I offered a residential weekend workshop on myth and culture at a small conference center outside Sydney, Australia. The meeting area was partially separated from another large space that we used for dancing and exercise. Huge warehouse doors provided the outside opening. We kept them resolutely closed; it was springtime there and chilly. During one break period (for tea, of course—this was Australia) I was sitting talking to a group of participants. My associate Peggy Rubin was standing with a small group of Aboriginal Coori women, over at one side. They could see the big doors across the open floor, though I could not.

Suddenly a little wagging dog of mixed lineage came pelting toward me and jumped into my lap, licking my face and generally implying, "Where have you been all my life!" I felt the same way, and we had a magnificent reunion of the heart, though I had never seen him before. He didn't belong to anyone there and we had no idea where he had come from or why. The dog's behavior didn't seem strange to me, for dogs and I live as old, dear friends and recognize each other easily and often—on the streets, in waiting rooms, in parking lots. After the break, I took the dog back outside and found its owner, who had been madly whistling for it. I went back to teaching and didn't give the incident any more thought.

Peggy, however, reported a different perspective on this visit from the dog world to the human workshop. She remembered the dog literally forcing his way into the room—vigorously scratching at the door until it swung outward far enough for his little body to squeeze in—then running pell-mell across the floor in a beeline for me. Knowing my familial relationship with dogs, she didn't think too much about it either, except to note that a sweet and insistent little creature had come in out of the cold.

The Aboriginal women's response, on the other hand, was much

199

different, Peggy told me. "They held their breath, and looked at one another in surprise, and at you, Jean, with new understanding and some awe," she related. "For them this wasn't ordinary. For them you had been claimed by one of their mythic ancestral beings, the dingo. 'Dingo Dreaming,' one of the women explained, 'is very powerful, and usually only men receive it.' I am so literal that I said, 'But this is just a dog, not a dingo,' and received a look of patient realization that I couldn't understand the truth that all dogs are descendants of the original Dingo."

The Dreaming, or Dreamtime, for an Aboriginal, is the ultimate ancestral space and time. They say that all creation was held in the Dreaming, and when the right moment came, ancestral beings, surging with energy, came forth to explore and create the landscape and bestow their gifts of life upon the earth. Each creature, tree, bush, pond holds spiritual power from that Aboriginal time. It is believed that human beings are related in the deepest possible sense to all living things, but most particularly to an individual species of plant or animal.

One is said to be part of Kangaroo Dreaming, or Wallaby, or Crocodile, or Paperbark Tree—or Dingo. These are one's literal, physical, spiritual, and emotional ancestors and present-day relations, and one shares responsibility with them for their well-being, their land's well-being, and one's own well-being. I have heard, for example, that a crocodile will never attack humans who are Crocodile Dreaming and that Dolphin Dreaming humans can call and communicate with dolphins. In other words, the relationship is powerful and alive and deep. In some languages, the word dreaming is translated as the "law." For all of these ancestors brought information about authentic ways humans can live together in mutual respect. The human spiritual journey requires that one go on a "walkabout" occasionally. This means that one travels the path of the ancestor while singing the songs taught about that path, thus restoring one's own inner balance and refreshing the spirit in the land itself.

The primary story about Dingo Dreaming concerns their journey as they traveled in pairs from far across the northern ocean to the continent of Australia. Reaching this hot, dry land, they traveled far and wide seeking water and creating water holes. As they dug vigorously for water, they also cast up groups of mountains and created rock and sand features in the landscape. Each part of Australia contains its own stories and myths concerning the dingo. Everywhere they are seen as friends and helpers, holders of the laws that inform their people of stories, songs, hunting tools, ceremonies. It is said that they learned and taught their descendants how to make fire, how to live happily as man and wife, how to respect others' stories and customs, and how to cooperate. And everywhere they are acknowledged as those who found the water, who were tireless in their efforts, casting back and forth across the huge land in search of the life-giving, life-restoring liquid.

I have too much respect for Aboriginal ways of knowing and understanding the deep world to dismiss my experience of being claimed by the archetypal Dingo as simply a little-lost-dog story. When Peggy reminded me of it, during the course of my writing this book, I felt a chill of recognition, yes, but also an awakened sense of responsibility. The Australian Aboriginals' connection to their landscape and to the creators of that landscape in the form of ancestors and relatives from the Dreamtime endows us with a rich way to pursue our spiritual journey and to honor Mother Earth at the same time.

When I review the words and work of this book in the light of Dingo Dreaming, I realize that I am saluting that mythic being who is also an ancestor, a relative, and a complete friend. And in my own way, I am fulfilling a part of my responsibility to my own Dreaming by inviting people to look at all animals, especially dogs, with fresh and respectful eyes.

The mythic dingoes knew the necessity for water and eagerly mapped an entire territory with locations of this essential substance so that all living beings could find their way to it. In the same way, my wonderful dogs have ceaselessly and insistently urged me to experience the bottomless spiritual waters that both source and resource my life. The best way to do that is to go on a walkabout following their footsteps, blessing the inner and outer landscapes they have touched while singing the songs they have created for me. This book is my walkabout and my Dreaming. I urge you to tell your own stories of life shared with beloved animals. In so doing, you may discover that many of life's deepest lessons have come through your "walkabout" with your animal friends. And who is to say who or what they really are?

An ancient story gives clues to the mystery of mystical dogs:

An old woman lived with her young son in a small village. She eked out a living for the two of them by working for her neighbors and by tending a single cow and some chickens. They were both deeply devout, the woman telling her son of the Buddha, the compassionate one, whose teaching relieved suffering. Painfully she saved tiny bits of money for the day her son would be old enough to go on pilgrimage to the very tree where the Buddha had gained enlightenment. He grew up, eagerly looking forward to the journey

At last the boy was old enough to make the trip, and there was enough money for him to travel the great distance and to buy a relic of the Buddha while in the holy city. "Bring me a tooth of the Buddha," his mother requested. "I have saved for this all my life and yours. Be very careful of the money. Here is just enough for you to live during the weeks you will be traveling, and the extra, this precious piece of gold, is for the tooth. Keep it safe in your packet." She kissed him and cried over him, and checked once again that his clothes (such as they were) were clean. She poured out all manner of instructions on him, as well as tears. "Don't forget the tooth," she reminded.

The boy, now a handsome young man, set out. Before very long he fell in with another group heading for the same place. There were all manner of people with the pilgrims, and they sang and chanted, making the journey a pleasant one.

Once in the city, however, the young man saw other things that looked attractive and soon forgot that he was on pilgrimage. What with one thing and another, all his money was soon gone, including the precious gold piece his mother had entrusted to him for the sacred relic, the Buddha's tooth. He woke up one morning with nothing left except a bad headache. He knew he had to find his way home somehow. And he was stricken with sorrow at how he had squandered his mother's money, so hard won. Hungry and thirsty, he began the painful trek back to his village without ever getting to the tree where the Buddha had reached enlightenment.

When night fell, the young man would lie down by the side of the road and sleep, exhausted and hungry, but still worrying about the relic he had been unable to buy. One morning, as he stumbled along the road, he saw an old dog that had died. As sometimes happens, the dog's mouth was slightly open and his teeth were showing. The young man reached in and touched one of the teeth. It fell out into his hand. He wrapped it in his torn loincloth.

When he finally arrived home, his mother was overjoyed beyond measure to see that he was alive and safe. And triply overjoyed when he presented her with the relic, "a tooth of the Buddha," as he declared it to be.

Sobbing with gratitude and awe, the mother washed the tooth

203

and placed it in the shrine she had prepared while the young man had been away. During the months and years that followed, the "relic" became a thing of incredible wonder to the villagers. In fact it almost became a reason for pilgrimage itself. Many miracles were attributed to it and to his mother as keeper of the Buddha's tooth. Her deeds of compassionate listening and goodness were profound and her happiness unbounded.

The young man, however, grew more and more distraught as the relic's reputation grew and his mother's saintliness increased. This built up over years, and finally he couldn't stand living a lie anymore. One evening, after several priests had visited and received both blessing and teaching from the tooth, he finally blurted out the true story to his mother. "That's not the Buddha's tooth. I lost all the money you gave me. I got that tooth from a dead dog!" And he ran outside the house.

Just outside the door stood a beautiful man looking at him with eyes of kindness and humor. It was the Buddha smiling. In a gentle voice, the Buddha said, "That was my tooth, you know."

NOTES

Introduction

1. Henry Beston, *The Outermost House: A Year of Life on the Great Beach of Cape Cod* (New York: Henry Holt, 1962), 24.

2. Rainer Maria Rilke, "Duino Elegies," in *The Selected Poetry of Rainer Maria Rilke*, ed. Stephen Mitchell (New York: Random House, 1982), 150.

Chapter 1

1. Jean Houston, *A Mythic Life: Learning to Live Our Greater Story* (San Francisco: HarperSanFrancisco, 1996), 65.

2. William Blake, "Auguries of Innocence," in *The Portable Blake* (New York: The Viking Press, 1962), 150.

3. Ibid., "The Marriage of Heaven and Hell," 258.

Chapter 2

1. *Further Dialogues with the Buddha,* vol. 1, trans. Lord Chalmers from the *Maijhima Nikaya* for the Pali Text Society (London: Oxford University Press, 1926), 56.

Chapter 3

1. Taigen Daniel Leighton, *Bodhisattva Archetypes: Classic Buddhist Guides to Awakening and Their Modern Expression* (New York: Arkana/Penguin, 1998), 2.

Chapter 4

1. Friedrich Nietzsche, *"Composition of Thus Spake Zarathustra,"* in *Ecce Homo*, trans. Clifton Fadiman. Cited in *The Creative Process,* ed. Brester Ghiselin (Berkeley: University of California Press, 1952), 137–138.

2. John O'Donohue, *Anam Cara: A Book of Celtic Wisdom* (New York: HarperCollins, 1997), 64.

Chapter 6

1. Kabir, trans. Rabindrath Tagore, in *Mystics, Masters, Saints and Sages* by Robert Ullman and Judith Reichenberg-Ullman (Berkeley, CA: Conari Press, 2001), 48.

2. Ibid., 49–50.

3. Kabir, in *The Mystic Vision* by Andrew Harvey and Anne Baring (San Francisco: HarperSanFrancisco, 1995), 49–50.

4. Marghanita Laski, *Ecstasy in Secular and Religious Experience* (Los Angeles: Jeremy Tarcher, Inc., 1976), 1.

5. Jean Houston, *A Passion for the Possible* (San Francisco: HarperSanFrancisco, 1997), 12.

6. William Wordsworth, "Lines Written a Few Miles Above Tintern Abbey," in *Poetical Works*, vol. 2, ed. Ernest de Selincourt (Oxford: Oxford University Press, 1952), 93–102.

Chapter 7

1. Evelyn Underhill, *Mysticism: The Nature and Development of Spiritual Consciousness* (Oxford: Oneworld Publications, 1999), 388–389.

2. Dylan Thomas, "The Force That Through the Green Fuse Drives the Flower," in *Chief Modern Poets of England and America*, vol. 1, ed. Gerald DeWitt Sanders, John Herbert Nelson, and M. L. Rosenthal (New York: The MacMillan Company, 1962), 410.

Chapter 8

1. These remarkable stories of union and reunion are found in *The Cults of the Dog* by M. O. Howey (Ashington, England: W. Daniel Co. Limited, 1972), 513–516. The second story, about the terrier who stole away to Japan in search of his master, originally appeared in the *Christian Science Monitor* in 1956.

2. Evelyn Underhill, *Mysticism: The Nature and Development of Spiritual Consciousness* (Oxford: Oneworld Publications, 1999), 426.

3. Ibid, 416.

4. Ibid, 414.

5. Ibid, 431.

6. T. S. Eliot, "Little Gidding," in *T. S. Eliot: The Complete Poems and Plays*, 1909–1950 (New York: Harcourt, Brace & World, Inc., 1952), 145.

7. Adapted from *"The Little Flowers of Saint Francis,"* trans. Raphael Brown (New York: Image Books, 1958), 88–91.

Inner Ocean Publishing

publishes in the genres of self-help, personal growth, lifestyle, conscious business, and inspirational nonfiction. Our goal is to publish books that touch the spirit and make a tangible difference in the lives of individuals, families, and their communities.

The six books in our Fall 2002 list reflect our company's goals, depict the process of personal growth and spiritual exploration that we cultivate in ourselves and others, and encourage a sense of personal responsibility in our individual, business, and global affairs. We invite you to visit us at:

www.innerocean.com.
Aloha.

Mystical Dogs:
Animals as Guides to Our Inner Life
by Jean Houston

In the High-Energy Zone:
The 6 Characteristics of Highly Effective Groups
by Paul Deslauriers

Sacred Selfishness:
A Guide to Living a Life of Substance
by Bud Harris, Ph.D.

Universal Water:
The Ancient Wisdom and Scientific Theory of Water
by West Marrin, Ph.D.

Choosing to Be Well:
A Conscious Approach to a Healthier Lifestyle
by Haven Logan, Ph.D.

The Gift of a Child
by Mary Ann Thompson